BACKSTAGE AT THE GRAND OLE OPRY

by

Dan Rogers

&

Brenda Colladay

Photography by Chris Hollo

Design by Catherine Hollo

GRANDIN HOOD
Publishers

Backstage at the Grand Ole Opry

Copyright © 2013 by Grand Ole Opry®, LLC
opry.com

The Grand Ole Opry wishes to acknowledge the following contributing photographers:
Les Leverett
Donnie Beauchamp
Joel Dennis
George Holz
Robin Hood

Published by Grandin Hood Publishers
1101 West Main Street
Franklin, Tennessee 37064
www.grandinhood.com

ISBN: 978-0-9838218-5-4

Endpaper images photographed from vintage letterpress woodblocks
courtesy of Hatch Show Print®, a Division of the Country Music Foundation, Inc.

Printed in China

Cover image: Opry member Dierks Bentley watches from the wings, ready to hit the stage.

WELCOME BACKSTAGE AT THE GRAND OLE OPRY!

While millions of fans have flocked to Nashville, Tennessee for nearly a century to witness the spectacle that is the Opry, relatively few have had the opportunity to walk the halls backstage, soaking in the magic that happens when generations of artists get together for a performance of the most famous show in country music. This book is that coveted backstage pass, taking readers behind the Opry's big red curtain and into the Opry House's dressing rooms, with other stops along the way including the Opry Member Gallery, musicians' room, and Family Room.

Thanks to all the artists and Opry staff members who have stopped for a photo or have taken a few minutes to tell us their great stories and memories from backstage now shared within these pages.

Thanks also to all the fans who tune in and drop by each week, thereby keeping the music playing onstage and ensuring that memorable Opry moments will continue not just on the stage, but backstage, too.

We hope you enjoy the (backstage) show!

Contents

Grand Ole Opry:
THE REAL SHOW IS BACKSTAGE

A Conversation with Garth Brooks

"**N**o offense at all to the people sitting in the seats, but the real show is backstage. That's the Opry," says superstar Grand Ole Opry member Garth Brooks.

For more than 85 years, millions of country music fans from around the world have visited the Opry and witnessed the magic of country music's greatest show. But for those like Brooks lucky enough to find themselves on the other side of the Opry's big red curtain, the show's backstage offers up even more timeless traditions, uproarious laughter, magical moments, and sometimes even more music than what is seen and heard under the bright lights center stage.

The rest of the Riders In The Sky stand clear as Oak Ridge Boy Duane Allen demonstrates his technique for "tickling the ivories" on Joey the CowPolka King's accordion.

"You're never gonna forget the first time you played at the Opry," Brooks says. "I was walking down the center hall getting ready to go out onstage. Me and Ty England, my best friend from college and guitar player. I look over as we're walking and Ty's face is paste-white. Whoa . . . I mean I was scared, but I was like 'Are you going to be OK?' Ty grits his teeth and whispers 'Look who is walking next to me.' I said 'What?' and he repeats 'Look who is walking next to me.' I look past his face and see the great Kitty Wells. And all of a sudden my face went paste-white. And all of a sudden it hits you where you are."

The utter fear of a newcomer to the Opry scene eventually gave way for Brooks to

: Brooks brings down the house during the Opry's 80th anniversary show in 2005. :

: Johnny Russell welcomes Brooks to the Opry family, October 6, 1990. :

a kind of familial kinship with others backstage. "So many memories," Brooks smiles. "I remember trying to make my way through the halls to get to the stage and Roy Acuff was signing autographs out of his dressing room, and a kid goes, 'Mr. Acuff, don't you wish you had a dollar for every autograph you signed?' And Roy never looked up, never missed a beat, and said, 'I do, son . . . I do.'"

"Then another time I was walking in with Whispering Bill [Anderson]. We are walking the back hall, the one that runs parallel to the stage, when around the corner comes Johnny Russell walking toward us. Johnny is wearing a white shirt with thin blue stripes going up and down it. Whispering Bill looks at him and goes, 'I have a mattress that looks just like you.'"

Like many of his fellow artists, several of Brooks' favorite backstage moments are musical in nature: "It was the Opry's 75th anniversary, and Johnny Russell, John Conlee, Whispering Bill, Porter [Wagoner], and I were going to rehearse 'Friends In Low Places.' There was a technical delay . . . I'm standing with a guitar, and John Conlee is sitting down on a stool to my right. I'm two feet away from him, and I just start plunking on that minor chord, singing the first couple of lines to his hit 'She Can't Say That Anymore.' He starts to grin, takes his microphone, raises it up to his mouth, and belts out the next line. And we took it from there. It was just one song after another, from 'Miss Emily's Picture' to 'I Don't Remember Loving

You' to 'Rose Colored Glasses' to 'Common Man.' These were all the songs I played in bars and clubs before I ever moved to Nashville. I laughed; I loved it. And the other guys were so magnanimous—they just sat and watched. It was unbelievable."

For Brooks and nearly everyone else who has made their way backstage at the Opry, the truly magical Opry moments occur when relationships formed backstage materialize on stage in front of an adoring audience.

Brooks recalls, "When Johnny Russell inducted us, we did 'Much Too Young.' When the song was over, the crowd would not stop clapping! I remember hanging my head and crying like a baby. Johnny came up to me and put his hand right square in the middle of the back of my neck and said, 'You enjoy it, son.'"

"It is one of the greatest memories of my life," Brooks says. "I love, love, love what that place stands for."

Johnny Russell, John Conlee, Garth Brooks, Bill Anderson, and Porter Wagoner perform an all-star version of Brooks' hit "Friends In Low Places" during the Opry's 75th anniversary special in 2000.

The Grand Ole Opry House

"There's no other stage that I've worked on, including Carnegie Hall, that can even compare with the Grand Ole Opry House. Not even close."
– Mel Tillis

Since 1974, the Grand Ole Opry House has welcomed country music's most celebrated artists and devoted fans to a venue and an experience like no other. More than a concert hall, it is the Opry family home, and as such, has hosted hundreds of special moments, and has even seen its share of trying times. In September 2010, the Opry House emerged from what had been undoubtedly the most challenging period in its history better and more welcoming than ever, ready to host country music's most famous show for generations to come.

FOUR FEET HIGH AND RISING

As the curtain rose and the packed house quieted, the strains of a century-old melody floated out to the audience. It was a song that had been performed hundreds of times on the Grand Ole Opry stage, but on this night, one of the most anticipated in the show's 85-year history, "Will the Circle Be Unbroken?" perfectly expressed the recent outpouring of emotion for country music's most cherished institution. A mere five months earlier, the Opry House stage with its iconic circle of wood taken from Ryman Auditorium was under nearly four feet of water, inundated by the historic May 2010 flooding that took 31 lives and destroyed billions of dollars in property across the region.

As soon as the news of the extensive damage at the Opry House became public, calls flooded in with condolences, concern, offers of help, and most passionate of all, the admonition that "the Opry must go on." And go on, it did. During the five months that the Grand Ole Opry House was closed for reconstruction, the show did not miss one performance. Artists, staff, and fans trekked from one end of Nashville to another, holding performances at War Memorial Auditorium and Ryman Auditorium (two of the show's former homes), neighboring Two Rivers Church, Municipal Auditorium, Tennessee Performing Arts Center's Jackson Hall, and Lipscomb University's Allen Arena.

Brad Paisley and Little Jimmy Dickens perform "Will the Circle Be Unbroken" on September 28, 2010, during *Country Comes Home: An Opry Live Celebration*, a show celebrating the post-flood reopening of the Grand Ole Opry House.

The Grand Ole Opry stage covered with nearly four feet of water, May 3, 2010

The door leading to the Opry stage, May 3, 2010

The Cumberland River inundates the Opry Plaza, May 3, 2010

Meanwhile, back at the Opry House, work progressed at an astounding pace. Opry staff and contractors worked around the clock, essentially demolishing and rebuilding much of the venue's interior and mechanical and technical infrastructure. The importance and significance of the Grand Ole Opry was the driving factor for everyone involved—they had to get the Opry back in the House. It was obvious as performances were staged elsewhere during the reconstruction that the Grand Ole Opry is the show, not the building. But it also became more evident than perhaps it had ever been that the Grand Ole Opry House, the show's venue since 1974—a venue that many locals still referred to as the "new" Opry House 35 years after it opened—is much more than just a building; it is a home.

A NEW COUNTRY HOME

As the Grand Ole Opry House was conceived and designed in the early 1970s, everyone from Opry management to Opry members to architects Welton Becket and Associates understood the magnitude of the undertaking: to create the first venue built specifically for performances of the Grand Ole Opry, nearly 50 years into the show's revered history. Of course, it would provide the modern technical facilities needed to produce the Opry and other live and televised shows, offer backstage amenities that the stars of the day were accustomed to, and include a comfortable auditorium for guests. But the functionality was the easy part of the job. The difficult part was to make the place feel like the home of the Opry.

Fans and artists worried. How would a big, fancy new building affect country music's most beloved institution? Bill Anderson heard the concerns from his fans. "Most of the fans out across the country who have expressed concern at the Opry's moving have been fearful that the Opry would 'change' . . . lose its 'color' . . . its homey atmosphere," he explained.

Worries were stoked by a controversial decision announced in 1971 by the Opry's parent company, National Life and Accident Insurance Company. Once the Grand Ole Opry House opened, Ryman Auditorium, the 1890s tabernacle that had been home to the Opry for nearly 30 years, would be demolished, and part of the building's remains would be used to construct a small chapel at the new Opryland site. As people weighed in from Nashville and across the country about saving the Ryman, the challenge of making

Pamphlet promoting the construction of the Grand Ole Opry House, 1973

the Grand Ole Opry House into a venue that could be loved by performers and guests alike became all the greater.

The Grand Ole Opry had landed at Ryman Auditorium on June 5, 1943, after jumping around Nashville from the WSM radio studios to a theater near Vanderbilt, to an austere tabernacle in East Nashville, to plush War

Memorial Auditorium—where the Opry and its rowdy crowds were invited to leave in 1943. The Ryman, a Victorian Gothic tabernacle in downtown Nashville, was terribly out-of-fashion architecturally and had few amenities for the performers or the audience: no dressing rooms, no air conditioning, and hard oak pew seating. But the venue, with its curved walls and aged wood had fabulous acoustics, and the rustic surroundings jelled with the "good-natured riot" the Opry brought into the 3,300-seat building.

The Opry thrived at the Ryman, and in order to accommodate overflow crowds, a Friday night show, a Saturday matinee, and a second Saturday night performance were added over time. But, by the mid-1960s, downtown Nashville was in decline. The Grand Ole Opry drew over 400,000 attendees

The Grand Ole Opry House under construction, 1972

each year, and management began to worry that the growingly seedy surroundings of Lower Broadway did not provide the family-friendly experience the Opry had always striven to present. Besides concern for the visitors' experience, the Opry leaders felt that they could no longer ask artists to perform in a theater without dressing rooms, and where the on-stage temperature during the summer could top 110 degrees. In a 1968 memorandum, National Life executive Irving Waugh proposed building a new venue for the Opry, arguing, "I am of the opinion that if we don't move to modernize our concept of the Opry operation, we will eventually lose that which has been such an institution." Plans for a new building were expanded to include a music-inspired theme park, Opryland U.S.A., and Opryland Hotel, a large hotel and convention center, to be located northeast of downtown Nashville.

Construction of the Grand Ole Opry House got underway on November 12, 1971. The design chosen for the building was in the architectural style known as "brutalism." The harsh-sounding name refers to the honesty and unpretentiousness of the style, where functional interior spaces are visible within the exterior form of the building, and where the building materials, such as concrete, brick, and rough-hewn wood are prominent, rather than concealed. Surrounding the Opry House, a beautifully landscaped plaza was designed to welcome guests with a lush display of flowers and foliage.

As work progressed, the challenge of pleasing the fans and artists who were apprehensive about moving to a new location continued to be of utmost concern. The Opry show had grown and changed organically over the decades, absorbing and reflecting new musical trends, styles, and artists, moving to new stages when required, and unabashedly displaying the casually organized chaos of a live radio show to its live audience. In the process, the show had become one of America's most distinctive and iconic entertainment experiences. But throughout the changing times, there remained an unbreakable connection to the traditions of the past—and that continuum was key to the Opry's future success as the new venue's architects and designers looked to the Opry's own attributes for inspiration. Grandeur could not trump warmth and familiarity, and elements from the Opry's past homes would be incorporated in meaningful ways.

Most visibly, the church pew seating for 4,400 fans hearkened back to the Ryman's origins as a tabernacle, though the new pews were padded—a welcome addition.

Backstage remained the gathering place that allowed Opry members to reunite each week, catching up on news, comparing notes from tours, and sharing the latest jokes from the road. But at the Opry House, there was plenty of room to spread out, make yourself at home, and stay a while.

The most inspired decision of all was to transport a six-foot circle of stage flooring from Ryman Auditorium to center stage at the Opry House. That simple yet powerful physical connection to tradition is deeply meaningful to artists and fans

alike, and has become a magical space for those who get the opportunity to stand in it. Opry member Alan Jackson says, "You think about people like Hank Williams, who stood on that spot of wood, and Mr. Acuff, and, of course, George Jones. And just about anybody you can think of who has made country music has been on that stage. That's what makes you so nervous—to think about the historical part of the Opry and how it's played such a part in country music." Trisha Yearwood swears, "You don't pass over that spot in the floor and not get a chill."

Roy Acuff and Opryland head Bud Wendell supervise as workers install the circle of Ryman stage flooring in the Opry House stage, 1974.

A TRULY GRAND OPENING

As construction neared completion, planning for the move to the Grand Ole Opry House took an exciting turn when it was announced that the president and first lady would be in attendance to dedicate the building during the March 16, 1974, opening, making it a grand opening indeed. No president had ever attended the Grand Ole Opry, and though President Richard Nixon was at the time embroiled in the Watergate scandal, it was an honor for the Opry, a sign of respect for country music, and a boon for Opry management, who knew the president's visit would guarantee massive press coverage for the Opry and its new $15 million home.

With the president's RSVP, the evening turned into an event that nobody wanted to miss, and one Nashville would never forget. On opening night, a standing-room-only crowd packed the Grand Ole Opry House. Luminaries in attendance included four governors (from Tennessee, Mississippi, Alabama, and New Mexico), three US senators (two from Tennessee and one from Indiana), and thirteen congressmen from across the country.

The show's opening segment delighted the audience. Film of a young Roy Acuff and his Smoky Mountain Boys from 1940 singing "Wabash Cannonball" was projected on a curtain that slowly rose to reveal Acuff and his band live on stage, picking up the song without missing a beat. But the real star of the show would hit the stage later and put on the performance of a lifetime.

A guitar, fiddle, and banjo version of "Hail to the Chief" greeted President Nixon as he walked onto the Opry stage. When the president pulled a bright

President Nixon makes his Opry debut, March 16, 1974.

First, country music is American. It started here, it is ours. It isn't something that we learned from some other nation, it isn't something that we inherited... Second, it relates to those experiences that mean so much to America. It talks about family, it talks about religion, the faith in God that is so important to our country and particularly to our family life. And as we all know, country music radiates a love of this Nation, patriotism... I wanted to take this opportunity on behalf of all the American people to thank country music, those who have created it, those who make it, those who now will have it continue in the future, for what it does to make America a better country, because your music does make America better. It is good for Americans to hear it. We come away better from having heard it.

: Roy Acuff gives a presidential yo-yo lesson. :

After the remarks, Acuff decided that the president needed one more chance at the yo-yo, and attempted to give the commander in chief a quick lesson. After another failed attempt, Nixon quipped, "I'll stay here and try to learn how to use the yo-yo; you go up and be President, Roy."

yellow yo-yo out of his pocket and let it dangle at the end of the string, confessing to renowned yo-yoist Acuff, "I haven't learned to use this thing yet," Acuff and the audience roared with laughter. Acuff then shepherded Nixon to the piano, where he played "Happy Birthday" and "My Wild Irish Rose" for the first lady, Pat Nixon, who happened to be celebrating her birthday that night.

Nixon moved from the piano to help unveil a dedicatory plaque and then back to the microphone where he spoke eloquently about country music. Among his comments:

In the extensive press coverage, even the most skeptical reporters admitted that President Nixon, often deemed cold and humorless, was perhaps more warm and relaxed at the Grand Ole Opry than Americans had ever seen him. It was a historic night for the Opry, and though other presidents have visited since, only Richard Nixon has the distinction of actually having *played* the Opry.

: Yo-yo used by President Nixon at the Opry House grand opening :
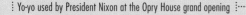

WHERE THE HEART IS

In the new, larger venue, attendance records were smashed, the show began airing as a weekly television series in 1985, and the Opry's reach grew larger than ever. The House became ground zero for country music programming as country music television specials, press conferences, decades of CMA Awards shows, and even Robert Altman's film, *Nashville*, took the stage. For new generations of aspiring country musicians, the Grand Ole Opry House became the place they dreamed of playing. So, it wasn't surprising when some of the Opry's youngest members were affected deeply by the damage from the 2010 flood.

Dierks Bentley told the press, "There's devastation all over the city. But to see the Grand Ole Opry affected, that just really hit home for me, even more than having water in my house." Blake Shelton also expressed his concern: "The Opry House is hallowed ground. We all need to help to make sure it lasts. I am devastated to hear that it is affected by this disaster."

The first Opry member to actually visit the Opry House in the wake of the flood was Brad Paisley,

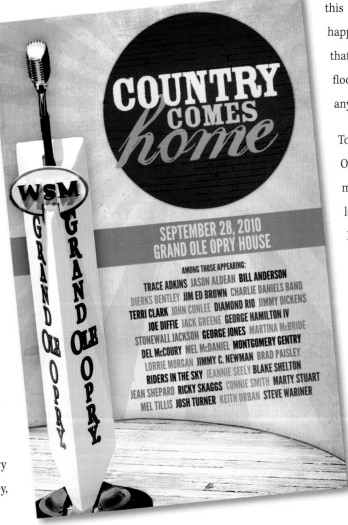

who led *NBC's Nightly News* team on a tour of the building. After seeing the extent of the damage, Paisley remarked, "I was born in the '70s so I grew up watching Bill Anderson host the *Opry Backstage* or Porter Wagoner, and seeing a guy like Jimmy Dickens bring on the show . . . And it's always been the Opry House. So much has happened in this building. My moments and my milestones happened here. And so . . . of all places, for me, that was the most heartbreaking thing about the flood. No personal loss of property to me came anywhere near."

Today, after the extensive restoration of the Opry House, the historic flood is but one of many stories shared backstage—another family legend to be passed along to new generations. Each week, the venue welcomes new artists and fans into the fold. And as they make their way to the stage to snap a photo, walk through the halls, kick back in a dressing room, or wait in the wings for the chance to stand in the famous circle, each makes new memories, creates a story of their own, and in the process, becomes a part of country music's biggest, most infamous and illustrious clan, the Grand Ole Opry.

The Opry cast holds a family reunion onstage during the *Country Comes Home* special on September 28, 2010.

Nothing Compares
BACKSTAGE AT THE GRAND OLE OPRY

by Bill Anderson

The stage from the Ryman balcony, 1956

Every auditorium, theater, and arena in the world has an area behind the stage where performers gather, dress, rehearse, and simply hang out before, during, and after their performances. And I have stood on hundreds of them.

But I've yet to see any such area that can even begin to compare to the professional frenzy that exists every weekend backstage at the Grand Ole Opry.

The first time I ever went to the Opry minus my parents, my high school buddies and I walked around to the far left side of the balcony in the old Ryman and spent a large portion of the evening mesmerized by the stars moving around and interacting with one another behind the backdrop.

I can still see Lonzo and Oscar sipping on R.C. Colas, at the time one of the Opry's primary sponsors. Comedian Rod Brasfield was walking around with a car tire tucked up under his arm. He would later use the tire as a prop during an onstage comedy routine with Minnie Pearl. George Morgan was engaged in pulling some kind of prank on Johnnie & Jack, and everyone was laughing themselves silly.

⋮ Bill Anderson poses backstage with a visiting disk jockey, Marion Worth, and Archie Campbell in 1964. ⋮

Years later, when I was first invited to make a few guest appearances on the Opry myself, I wondered at the maze of musicians, singers, dancers, announcers, and stage hands who seemed to be aimlessly wandering around backstage, yet somehow managing to keep the unscripted show running and on time.

Once I became an Opry member myself, I came to understand it better, but I never ceased to wonder at it all. Roy Acuff, the King of Country Music himself, would sit casually with his dressing room door open, inviting fans to come in and talk with him and take pictures, and yet Mr. Roy insisted on rehearsing our duet, "I Wonder If God Likes Country Music," each and every time before we sang it onstage.

Hank Snow would pack his band into a tiny, hot dressing room backstage at the Ryman to rehearse songs like "I'm Movin' On," which he had obviously performed hundreds, if not thousands, of times. Bill Monroe was constantly playing his mandolin and singing those high, lonesome bluegrass tunes to only a handful of fellow musicians.

One day it hit me. For all the apparent confusion and turmoil backstage, these performers were much like professional athletes who talk about "getting their game faces on" before a big contest. They always wanted to be ready to give their fans their very best, and that's why they always did.

: Steve Wariner, Bill Anderson, and Brad Paisley backstage at the Opry House, 2001 :

And yet, away from the footlights, there was always such a human side to it all. Minnie Pearl never left the building until she had walked the main hallway and told her friends goodnight. I can still hear her reassuring voice saying, "Goodnight, Bill Anderson. I love you."

There are now mammoth pictures of both Miss Minnie and Mr. Roy hanging just inside the artist entrance to the Opry. Every night as I leave the building,

I look up at those photographs and say goodnight to them both.

"Goodnight, Minnie Pearl," I always say out loud. "I love you too."

And every time I say it I just can't help but think to myself there simply will never be anything to compare with the pure magic that exists backstage at the Grand Ole Opry.

ARTIST ENTRANCE

It could be called the place where the butterflies begin. It isn't a long walk from the back parking lot to the artist entrance lobby at the Grand Ole Opry House, but it is a momentous one. Lined with flowers and star-shaped boxwoods, the "star walk," as some like to call it, represents the final few steps in a lifelong dream. The path deposits performers at the Artist Entrance to the Grand Ole Opry House, where any doubts that they are in the right place are dispelled as they are greeted by six-foot photographs of the Opry's beloved cast members, Roy Acuff and Minnie Pearl.

Next, they proceed to the check-in desk where all performers and backstage guests must stop and make sure they are "on the list." A second round of butterflies is calmed when the name is located and performers are directed to their dressing rooms for the evening.

Opry security officer Jim Vanderstyne checks to make sure backstage visitors are "on the list."

Charlie Daniels' tour bus parked alongside the backstage entrance "star walk" gives Opry newcomers something to aspire to.

The artist entrance lobby

Minnie Pearl
FOUNTAIN

Sarah Ophelia Colley Cannon, known to fans the world over as Minnie Pearl, bequeathed this lovely bronze fountain featuring a sculpture of a young girl at a water fountain to the Grand Ole Opry. The fountain, which now greets visitors along the walk to the Opry House artist entrance, was a gift from her husband, Henry Cannon.

A WWII Army Air Corps pilot, Cannon swept Sarah "Ophie" Colley off of her feet when he declared, "Baby, after the Lord made you he sure must have buffed his nails," and proposed marriage before they had even had a proper date. The two married on February 23, 1947, and Cannon and his trusted DC-3 aircraft soon began flying Minnie and her Opry co-stars to show dates across America, extending the distance performers could travel during the week and still make it back for their mandatory Saturday night Opry spots. Henry Cannon was a fixture at the Grand Ole Opry, and known for his dry sense of humor. Minnie once commented admiringly, "He thinks funny. He has a dry wit and his timing is absolutely perfect"—high praise from one of America's most beloved comediennes. The pair were inseparable until Sarah's death on March 4, 1996. Henry passed away on November 7, 1997.

Henry and Sarah Cannon

"This little fountain is an original sculpture by the late Jesse Beasley —one of the very few that he created. It is a very cherished piece given to me by my husband on our twenty-fifth wedding anniversary."
— Sarah Cannon

Special Delivery!
GRAND OLE OPRY POST OFFICE

After checking in at the security desk, one of the first stops for Opry members on show nights is the eye-catching Grand Ole Opry Post Office. A tradition carried over from the days at Ryman Auditorium, each Grand Ole Opry member is assigned a post office box, and fans can easily send letters or packages to their favorite member in care of the Opry.

The boxes are assigned to members in alphabetical order—with one exception. Alphabetically, Little Jimmy Dickens should find his mail on the top row of boxes—right between Diamond Rio and Joe Diffie. But that would be a stretch for the 4'11" entertainer, so his box is number 144, located in the fourth row down.

One favorite Opry Post Office story demonstrates the renown of the Grand Ole Opry (and one of its beloved icons). Country music songwriter and disc jockey Joe Allison once mailed a letter to Minnie Pearl from Los Angeles with nothing but a sketch of her famous hat for an address. In short order, it arrived at the Grand Ole Opry.

There's no guarantee a drawing will get the mail delivered, but to reach the Opry Post Office, write any current member in care of:

Grand Ole Opry
2804 Opryland Drive
Nashville, TN 37214

OPRY PHILATELY

Several country music artists who have performed on the Opry stage have been featured on US postage stamps, as has the historic Ryman Auditorium. The most recent addition, a stamp honoring Johnny Cash, was unveiled June 5, 2013.

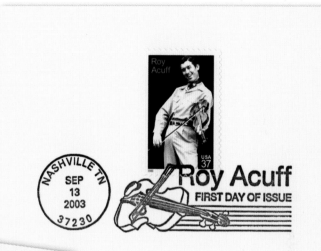

Roy Acuff stamp issued in 2003

Ryman Auditorium stamped postcard issued in 2000

"Legends of American Music" stamps issued in 1993

Wall of Fame
OPRY MEMBER GALLERY

Many Opry traditions can be traced back decades, but Blake Shelton began a brand-new one the night of his induction, October 23, 2010. After being introduced as the newest member of the Opry cast, Blake took it upon himself to personally add his name to the Opry Member Gallery, a display featuring individual plaques engraved with the names of more than 200 artists and groups who have been members of the Opry since 1925.

The plaques are arranged chronologically, beginning in 1925 with the Opry's first featured performer, Uncle Jimmy Thompson, and ending with the most recent inductee—with plenty of empty spots for new members to be added, of course. Anxious to place his name alongside his Opry heroes, Shelton took over the duties with a screwdriver and attached the bronze plaque. Every new member since then has followed Blake's example, including Keith Urban, who made use of a pocketknife Marty Stuart had given him earlier that night to add his plaque to the gallery.

The Oak Ridge Boys, shown here on their induction night, joined the Opry cast on August 6, 2011, after decades of performing as guests.

OPRY MEMBERS

Uncle Jimmy Thompson

Dr. Humphrey Bate and his Possum Hunters

Uncle Dave Macon

Henry Bandy

Mazy Todd

The Pickard Family

DeFord Bailey

The Crook Brothers

Sid Harkreader

Theron Hale and his Daughters

The Binkley Brothers and their Dixie Clodhoppers

Sam and Kirk McGee

Arthur Smith

The Fruit Jar Drinkers

W. Ed Poplin and his Barn Dance Orchestra

Kitty Cora Cline

Uncle Jo Magrum and Fred Schriver

The Gully Jumpers

The Vagabonds

Zeke Clements

Asher and Little Jimmie Sizemore

The Delmore Brothers

The Lakeland Sisters

Robert Lunn

Nap and Dee

Leroy "Lasses" White

Sarie and Sally

Jack Shook and his Missouri Montaineers

Pee Wee King and his Golden West Cowboys

Curly Fox and Texas Ruby

Roy Acuff and his Smoky Mountain Boys

The Tennessee Valley Boys

Hilltop Harmonizers

Jamup and Honey

The Andrews Brothers

Bill Monroe and his Blue Grass Boys

Ford Rush

John Daniel Quartet

Paul Howard and his Arkansas Cotton Pickers

Minnie Pearl

David "Stringbean" Akeman

The Duke of Paducah (Whitey Ford)

Bradley Kincaid

Curley Williams and his Georgia Peach Pickers

Ernest Tubb

Eddy Arnold

Pete Pyle and his Mississippi Valley Boys

The Bailes Brothers

The Cackle Sisters (Carolyn and Mary Jane Dezurik)

Clyde Moody

The Poe Sisters

Rod Brasfield

Lew Childre

The Old Hickory Singers

The Tennessee Sweethearts (Clyde and Marie Dilleha)

Wally Fowler and his Georgia Clodhoppers

Grandpa Jones

Red Foley

The Willis Brothers

Annie Lou and Danny Dill

Milton Estes and his Musical Millers

Johnnie and Jack

Lonzo and Oscar

Cowboy Copas

Jimmy Dickens

George Morgan

The Jordanaires

Hank Williams

Hank Snow

Cedar Hill Square Dancers

Cousin Jody (James Clell Summey)

Chet Atkins

Mother Maybelle Carter and the Carter Sisters

Moon Mullican

Lefty Frizzell

Ray Price

Carl Smith

Ralph Sloan and his Tennessee Travelers

Martha Carson

Faron Young

Kitty Wells

Webb Pierce

Marty Robbins

Goldie Hill

The Wilburn Brothers

The Ladells

Benny Martin

The Carlisles (Bill Carlisle)

Del Wood

Ferlin Husky

Red Sovine

Slim Whitman

The Louvin Brothers

Hawkshaw Hawkins

Hank Thompson

Justin Tubb

Jim Reeves

Jean Shepard

Johnny Cash

Jimmy C. Newman

George Jones

Rose Maddox

Stonewall Jackson

Lester Flatt and Earl Scruggs

Wilma Lee and Stoney Cooper

Porter Wagoner

The Everly Brothers

Rusty and Doug Kershaw

Archie Campbell

Don Gibson

Carl and Pearl Butler

Roy Drusky

Ben Smathers and the Stoney Mountain Cloggers

Billy Grammer

Margie Bowes

Skeeter Davis

Billy Walker

Patsy Cline

The Glaser Brothers

Bobby Lord

Hank Locklin

George Hamilton IV

Bobby Bare

Bill Anderson

Charlie Walker

Merle Travis

Jimmy Driftwood

Loretta Lynn

Leroy Van Dyke

Sonny James

Marion Worth

Norma Jean

The Browns

Jim and Jesse

Ernie Ashworth

Dottie West

The Osborne Brothers

Willie Nelson

Tex Ritter

Bob Luman

Connie Smith

Ray Pillow

Del Reeves

The Four Guys

Stu Phillips

Jeannie Seely

Jack Greene

Dolly Parton

Tammy Wynette

Tom T. Hall

Jan Howard

David Houston

Barbara Mandrell

Jeanne Pruett

Jerry Clower

Ronnie Milsap

Don Williams

Larry Gatlin and the Gatlin Brothers

Melvin Sloan Dancers

John Conlee

Boxcar Willie

B.J. Thomas

Ricky Skaggs

Riders In The Sky

The Whites

Lorrie Morgan

Johnny Russell

Mel McDaniel

Reba McEntire

Randy Travis

Roy Clark

Ricky Van Shelton

Patty Loveless

Holly Dunn

Mike Snider

Garth Brooks

Clint Black

Alan Jackson

Vince Gill

Emmylou Harris

Travis Tritt

Marty Stuart

Charley Pride

Alison Krauss

Joe Diffie

Hal Ketchum

Bashful Brother Oswald (Beecher Ray Kirby)

Martina McBride

Steve Wariner

Johnny Paycheck

Diamond Rio

Trisha Yearwood

Ralph Stanley

Pam Tillis

Brad Paisley

Trace Adkins

Del McCoury

Terri Clark

Dierks Bentley

Mel Tillis

Josh Turner

Charlie Daniels

Carrie Underwood

Craig Morgan

Montgomery Gentry

Blake Shelton

Oak Ridge Boys

Rascal Flatts

Keith Urban

Darius Rucker

Old Crow Medicine Show

Little Big Town

"Checking in backstage, getting my dressing room and finding out what room I'm in that night. My favorite dressing room is #5, 'Stars And Stripes.' Having been a member of the Service for a long time makes it a special room for me."

"This is awesome. Every time I walk into the backstage, I reach up and touch the Grand Ole Opry sign. There are football teams that touch a statue before they walk out on to the field. That's our statue."

"We were recording some acoustic stuff backstage here. The Opry is a great place for us to record and do all kinds of special projects. I've done three or four specials for CNN, filming for my TV show, and lots of other specials."

WITH *Craig Morgan*

"Signing autographs for the fans backstage. You never know who you'll see at the Opry. I've met President Bush a few times and saw him once at the Opry and I remember being extremely impressed that he remembered my name."

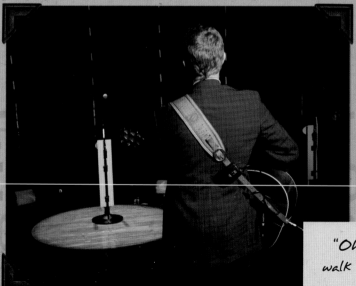

"Oh my gosh! This is me right before you walk on stage to stand in that special circle. I always enter from stage right."

"Finishing up a set and walking off stage. Thank you! It's very humbling to be doing a show on the Grand Ole Opry and look over to some of the artists I grew up listening to standing on the side of the stage. Jimmy Dickens, John Conlee, and Jim Ed Brown. George Jones had a birthday celebration here, and we came on and sang George Jones songs. I'll never forget standing there looking over at George singing one of his songs. He said, 'Son, you're gonna be a big star some day.' Now that was pretty dang cool!"

Feels Like Home
OPRY HOUSE DRESSING ROOMS

With upwards of 80 artists, musicians, and dancers performing on any given night at the Opry, the Grand Ole Opry House needs plenty of dressing rooms. To meet this need, the venue has 18 backstage dressing rooms to hold the masses of talented performers before they hit the stage. These are not, however, like any other dressing rooms in any other venue. To walk through them is to walk through Grand Ole Opry history, illustrated with hundreds of photographs and filled with warm, welcoming furnishings that enhance the homelike feel of the space.

After the May 2010 flood, the Opry House required complete reconstruction of the backstage areas. During this process, the dressing rooms were transformed into unique spaces inspired by the story of the Opry, each designed to tell a part of the story through décor, artwork, and a unique name.

In the wake of the flood, Nashville interior designer Kathy Anderson got the call to design the new spaces. She knew the job, however daunting, was for her. "I grew up listening to the Opry. I love the Opry. I respect the artists . . . and I get it." Anderson and her team at Anderson Design Studio set about creating rooms to reflect Opry-related themes such as "Into the Circle," "Bluegrass," "It Takes Two," "Cousin Minnie," and "Star & Stripes." The one dressing room not found is #13, as superstition dictates that the "unlucky" number be skipped.

A local graphic design firm, Anderson Design Group (no relation!), created artwork for each of the dressing room doors that reflects the room's theme. In an incredibly short timeline of five months, the renovations were completed, and the dressing rooms now beautifully illustrate the story of the Grand Ole Opry. The Opry artists were thrilled with the outcome, as Anderson explains, "The new artists think it is hip and cool, and the older artists like that it gives respect to the Opry."

Backstage at the Opry House has always been a place people have dreamed about, and now, the reality lives up to the dream. As Brad Paisley commented upon seeing the renovations, "They've made this a place where the backstage is going to be just as much fun as the front, and that is what this is all about."

Each dressing room is numbered with an oversized guitar pick inlaid in the floor in front of the door.

George Jones visits with Roy Acuff in his dressing room. Jones often recalled how when he was a child, if he fell asleep before Acuff's Opry performance on Saturday nights, his mother would always wake him up so he could be sure to hear his favorite singer.

The brass plaque, placed on the door of dressing room #1 by the King of Country himself, reads, "Ain't nothing gonna come up today that me and the good Lord can't handle." It's a sentiment that reflects the unflappable nature of a man who welcomed US presidents, entertainment icons, and legions of fans through that always-open door—and greeted each with the same warmth and familiarity.

Joining the Grand Ole Opry cast in 1938, Roy Acuff prided himself on giving the folks a show. He kept audiences rapt during his emotional, sometimes even tearful performances of sentimental songs like "Great Speckled Bird" or "Wreck on the Highway." Then, he would have them rolling with laughter as his band, The Smoky Mountain Boys, cut up and clowned their way through "Night Train to Memphis" and "Wabash Cannonball" as Acuff stole the spotlight performing yo-yo tricks and balancing his fiddle on his chin.

Acuff played this fiddle during his 1937 Opry debut.

"I love this stage.

You can let this curtain

fly back and I'm ready."

For over 18 years, dressing room #1 was Mr. Roy's home away from home. The décor reflects the feel of the rich, dark-paneled study of his former home in the Opry Plaza, just northwest of the Opry House. Over the caramel-colored leather sofa hangs a display of photographs highlighting special moments from Acuff's storied 54-year career with the Opry.

John Hartford soaks up some old-time picking from Roy Acuff and Smoky Mountain Boy Gene Martin in dressing room #1, September 2, 1978.

In 1981, a street in Nashville's famed Music Row area was named after Acuff, seen here posing with Nashville mayor Richard Fulton at the unveiling.

Roy Acuff and his Smoky Mountain Boys pose in dressing room #1 in 1975. Pictured L to R: Howard "Howdy" Forrester, Gene Martin, Roy Acuff, Jimmy Riddle, Charlie Collins, Onie Wheeler, Pete "Bashful Brother Oswald" Kirby

Roy Acuff and his Smoky Mountain Boys pose in WSM Studio B about 1947. Pictured L to R: Lon "Pap" Wilson, Jess Easterday, Rachel Veach, Roy Acuff, Pete "Bashful Brother Oswald" Kirby

The Door Is Always Open...

"For some reason Mr. Roy was really taken with me," Vince Gill recalls. "He loved 'When I Call Your Name.' He always made me sing that every time I was on his show. One of my most precious possessions is a photograph of me singing with Mr. Roy looking on. He couldn't see very well, so he was right there beside me, and he had tears in his eyes. That meant the world to me—that whatever music I was making spoke to him, you know? Around that time the two of us sat in here [dressing room #1] for three or four hours, and he confided so many stories to me that I have never told a soul."

FROM "MR. ROY" TO VINCE GILL

Vince Gill never asked to inherit dressing room #1, the room in which Opry patriarch Roy Acuff held court from the Opry House's opening in 1974 until his death in 1992. Gill says, "For years I'd walk in [the backstage entrance] and I'd say, 'Where ya got me tonight?' and they'd say, 'number one.' I never took it for granted."

But to fellow Opry stars, staff, and backstage guests, it's altogether fitting that the Opry member who has gone on to join "Mr. Roy" in the Country Music Hall of Fame should occupy that fabled real estate whenever he makes an Opry appearance. Though their time as fellow Opry members was limited to just over a year, the bond between the two Opry pillars lives on today. Nearly anyone who has met Gill backstage would agree he's a joyful embodiment of the words on Acuff's door: "Ain't nothing gonna come up today that me and the Lord can't handle."

"The most important thing I remember about Roy and this room is that the door was always open," Gill says while sitting in the dressing room after an Opry performance. "If he was here, I never saw this door closed. Everybody was welcome. There was always a jam session going on, and I kind of liked that chaotic thing. It spoke to me in a big way."

Gill fully embraces the King of Country Music's long tradition of keeping dressing room #1's door open, welcoming friends and fans for a backstage jam or friendly hello.

"Amy [wife Amy Grant] loves to tell a story about a night after Roy had gone on," Gill says. "We had long-finished the show, and there was this old fiddler in here who said, 'Can we play one?' I said, 'Sure, man, get your fiddle out.' So he got his fiddle out of his case and we played three or four songs."

"Then when we were riding home, Amy said, 'That was so cool and so much fun how that last guy, that old fiddler, played with you. He must be a real legend for you to sit and play with him like that.'"

"I looked over at her and said, 'I have no idea who that guy was. I've never met him before.'"

"She said, 'You're kidding,' and I said, 'Nope; I've never seen him before.'"

"That's the true magic of this place to me."

Though people assume bluegrass music is as old as the hills, the Grand Ole Opry stage is actually where the genre was born. Kentucky singer, songwriter, and mandolinist William Smith Monroe joined the Opry cast in 1939 with his string band, The Blue Grass Boys. His music was perfectly suited for the Opry—rooted in tradition, but performed with a modern twist. After hearing him audition, Opry founder George D. Hay declared that if Monroe ever wanted to leave the cast, he'd have to fire himself.

Bill Monroe experimented with his sound and tinkered with his lineup until landing on a magical combination in late 1945 when two key Blue Grass Boys—Tennessee-born guitarist and singer Lester Flatt and North Carolina native and innovative banjo virtuoso Earl Scruggs—joined the group and helped Monroe find his signature sound. Along with bass player Cedric Rainwater and fiddler Chubby Wise, the lineup is considered to be the original bluegrass band. Bluegrass is now played all over the world, and remains a staple of the Grand Ole Opry with a full slate of bluegrass artists as members and frequent guests.

Pickin' on the Opry stage are Vince Gill, Earl Scruggs, Ricky Skaggs, Roy Huskey Jr., Marty Stuart, and Alison Krauss, April 2, 1994.

Bluegrass greats gather backstage at the Ryman in 1973. Back row L to R: James Monroe, Mac Wiseman, Bill Yates, Ralph Stanley, Jimmy Martin; Front row L to R: Don Reno, Bill Monroe, Lester Flatt

Del McCoury was a member of Bill Monroe's band in the 1960s. Today, he leads his own group that includes his two sons. Their inspired covers of pop, rock, and blues songs have helped introduce bluegrass to new generations of fans. The Del McCoury Band, clockwise from center back: Del McCoury, Alan Bartram, Rob McCoury, Ron McCoury, Jason Carter

The design of dressing room #2 is inspired by the acoustic instruments that make up a bluegrass band. Alternating planks of light and dark wood flooring represent strings and frets, and the warm light brown tones of the walls and sofa call to mind the finish of a well-seasoned flat-top guitar. Photographs of all the bluegrass artists who have been Opry members line the walls. The room is furnished with several straight-backed armless chairs that are just perfect for sittin' and pickin'.

Bill Monroe poses with the Blue Grass Boys at WSM, c. 1940.

Ricky Skaggs and his band, Kentucky Thunder, warm up for the Opry.

Sponsor Martha White Flour helped Flatt & Scruggs travel in style.

His signature songs, "A Sleepin' at the Foot of the Bed," "Take an Old, Cold Tater and Wait," and "Out Behind the Barn," give a glimpse into what life was like growing up as the youngest of 13 children in a Bolt, West Virginia, coal mining family. But "Little" Jimmy Dickens was destined for big things.

Dickens first played the Grand Ole Opry as a guest of Roy Acuff, and joined the cast in 1948. He toured the globe as the first country artist to embark on a "round the world" tour and has appeared in countless television shows and music videos. In 2010 he celebrated his 90th birthday on the Opry stage.

During his decades-spanning career, Dickens has performed alongside country music's most renowned artists. He received comedy coaching from none other than Minnie Pearl, and has counted among his best friends and fishing buddies the likes of Hank Williams, Waylon Jennings, and Brad Paisley. Little Jimmy is true country music royalty, having been inducted into the Country Music Hall of Fame in 1983.

4'11" Little Jimmy Dickens scaled a kitchen ladder on June 14, 2003 in order to be eye to eye with 6'6" Trace Adkins when inviting the Louisiana native to become an official Opry member.

Jimmy Dickens and Brad Paisley take the stage in 2007. Brad has enlisted his good friend and fellow West Virginian as a guest star for several recordings and music videos.

"I think the Grand Ole Opry will go down in the history books as one of the greatest shows that has ever been."

Dressing room #3 is inspired by the fun and humor Jimmy brings to the Opry stage, and by the colorful sparkle of his rhinestone suits. A low, sleek, black and silver metallic sofa lines one wall while a pair of bright green calf hair upholstered chairs sit opposite. Mirrored tables and silver accents lend extra sparkle, and the walls hold large canvas art prints created from close-up photographs of Jimmy's own custom-made stage wear.

Dickens gives it his all at an April 1956 *Friday Night Frolic*. Pictured L to R: Jimmy "Spider" Wilson, George McCormick, Goldie Hill, Dickens, Joel Price

Jimmy listens along with Opry announcer Grant Turner and Opry star Red Foley while the great Hank Williams plays them one of his future classics during a 1949 tour of American military bases in Europe.

Looking dapper at the WSM microphone in a 1950s publicity shot

Jimmy chases June Carter across the Opry stage, 1956.

"What I remember now about my first Opry performance was waiting in the wings to go on and seeing the WSM sign on the microphone. Then a surreal walk to the mic and standing in the famous circle. I kept thinking 'this is not a place "like" the Opry, it IS the Opry and I'M PLAYING ON STAGE!' Crazy . . . I guess in a lot of ways being backstage for the first time felt just like I hoped it would. Timeless, magical, and rich in music and stories. It really is quite surreal, I gotta say!"
– Keith Urban

Stepping for the first time onto the six-foot circle of well-worn, 2-inch oak planks—a section taken from the stage of the historic Ryman Auditorium and inlaid front and center of the Grand Ole Opry House stage—represents the culmination of years of work, practice, sacrifice, and faith. The nerves and emotions brought on by an invitation to play the Opry are deep—tied up in family and tradition, in fulfillment of an artist's personal dream, and in realizing that they've "made it." The circle is a perfect symbol of the continuum that artists join. They are a small part of something bigger and more lasting than a hit song or a record-breaking tour—they are part of the Opry story.

Pistol Annies, September 25, 2012

Members of Lady Antebellum chat with Bill Anderson the night of their Opry debut, June 29, 2007.

"I was on cloud nine,
standing there singing
a song of mine,
standing where Johnny
Cash, Marty Robbins,
Ernest Tubb, Hank
Williams, Patsy Cline,
and Roy Acuff had stood."

I could die tomorrow and I've already been in heaven. I remember coming to the Opry and watching Loretta when I was 17. I was standing in the front row hoping and dreaming I'd be there someday, and tonight, she's going to be in the front row listening to me sing one of her songs. I'm just so tickled to be here. This is it for me."

- Angaleena Presley of Pistol Annies before their Opry debut on Loretta Lynn's 50th Opry anniversary show, September 25, 2012

"Along with Al Green and playing at the Apollo Theatre, it was one of the three greatest musical moments of my life."

- Darius Rucker, July 15, 2008

"Oh my God, I'm on the Opry!"

- Taylor Swift, September 1, 2006

Into the Circle, a tribute to Opry debuts, is designed to be warm and welcoming with soft and comfortable velvet-upholstered furniture on which to sit and contemplate—or maybe faint if needed! The walls feature photographs of artists making their debuts and a selection of memorable quotes regarding "the first time."

⋮ Darius Rucker ⋮

⋮ Taylor Swift ⋮

⋮ Lorrie Morgan makes her Grand Ole Opry debut at age 14 in 1973 as her father, Opry member George ⋮
⋮ Morgan, watches proudly. That night she thought, "This is what I'm going to do for the rest of my life." ⋮

"...these superstars I had been idolizing for years like Ernest... kind of like an amateur going on for my first talent show."

Jimmy Dickens, 1948

"Until I started playing the Opry, I didn't realize how powerful it is. The first time I played it I felt a real power - the power of heritage, of tradition, of the written word."

Hal Ketchum, 1991

"I thought, 'This is what I'm going to do for the rest of my life.'"

Lorrie Morgan, 1973

"Along with Al Gre... at the Apollo Theatre, it was one of the... musical moments of my life."

Darius R...
July 15, 2008

JOSH TURNER'S STORIED OPRY DEBUT

Josh Turner's Grand Ole Opry debut in December 2001 has become somewhat legendary in Opry storytelling circles. "When the curtain opened that night," a narrator might begin, "no one holding a ticket to the show had ever heard of Josh Turner. But by the end of that chilly Nashville evening, the young singer was all anyone in the audience could talk about."

Longtime Opry member Bill Anderson introduced Turner to the audience that night, then stepped across the stage to watch the youngster deliver his song. "I walked over to the podium and watched as he sang the song about the long black train [Turner's self-penned "Long Black Train," the tune that would become his first hit]," Anderson later recalled. "He had Tommy White, the steel guitar player in the Opry band, playing the Dobro, and the audience just got almost eerily quiet. I mean it was one of those things where you knew they were really listening to this young kid who was making his first Opry appearance. Josh's voice, and that song, and that Dobro—the combination of those three things—was absolutely mesmerizing . . . This kid just absolutely had them in the palm of his hand."

The eerie quiet Anderson described turned to thunderous applause and a standing ovation before Turner had even reached the second verse of his song. "Oh, man," Turner recalls, "before and after the performance is a blur.

But when I was out there on stage, that moment is forever engrained in my mind. I'll never forget it. They were cheering for the music. They started clapping and stomping, and I kept thinking to myself, 'Don't forget the words. Don't forget the words.' Then they started hollering and I thought, 'Lord, get me through this song.'"

Brad Paisley was on hand that night and reflected on the phenomenon he witnessed. "Man, I was so overwhelmed by the response," Paisley recalled. "I think in our industry sometimes we get real jaded about what it takes to get a crowd to go nuts. You know, we associate things like jumping around and cheerleading and all those things that happen out there on the stage as the kind of things that make the crowd get whipped into a frenzy. And all of a sudden, here comes Josh. I'm standing on the side of the stage, and he walks out and he sings this gospel song with his bass voice. He's so unassuming, and he was so humble out there. And the next thing you know, the crowd, I think, associated themselves with him in a way that they hadn't associated themselves with anybody all night. They saw a real guy out there singing a real song."

Being called back for an encore during which the audience rewarded him with another standing ovation cemented the night in Turner's memory forever. "I was fighting back the tears out there," he said. "I couldn't think straight. I was tore up."

The Stars & Stripes dressing room pays tribute to America's fighting forces, celebrates the Grand Ole Opry's long-standing relationship with them, and expresses gratitude for their service.

Even before the US entered WWII, the Grand Ole Opry had established its close relationship with the men and women of our armed forces. A group of Opry entertainers including Pee Wee King, Minnie Pearl, and Eddy Arnold formed a touring troupe known as the Camel Caravan. The troupe carried the sounds of country music to soldiers stationed at Army bases in the United States and Central America.

During WWII, the Opry provided a welcome dose of home for troops fighting overseas, as it was broadcast over the Armed Forces Radio Network, where it is still carried today.

Countless Opry members, including Roy Acuff, Jimmy Dickens, Ernest Tubb, Jeannie Seely, John Conlee, and Craig Morgan, have appeared in USO shows—in Germany, Korea and Vietnam, Bosnia, Iraq, and everywhere in between—logging thousands of miles to entertain the men and women who defend America at home and abroad.

In recognition of his commitment to America's troops and veterans, Charlie Daniels was named an honorary brigadier general in the Tennessee National Guard. The honor was bestowed during Charlie's 75th birthday celebration at the Opry.

Hank Snow and band perform for American troops in Korea, March 1953.

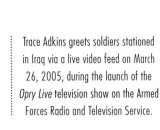

Trace Adkins greets soldiers stationed in Iraq via a live video feed on March 26, 2005, during the launch of the *Opry Live* television show on the Armed Forces Radio and Television Service.

On the home front, the Grand Ole Opry has partnered with many organizations in support of members of the military and its veterans, including America Supports You, the Wounded Warrior Project, and The Honor Flight Network.

Old Glory takes center stage in dressing room #5 with a wall-sized mural of a weathered American flag. The distressed leather sofa sports handmade needlepoint flag motif pillows. Subtle red, white, and blue accents are found in the rug, upholstered chairs, and accessories. A favorite element with guests, a striking brass eagle lamp keeps watch over the room. Framed posters and photos depict many of the initiatives the Opry has been involved in over the years in support of our troops.

Roy Acuff, Whitey Ford (the Duke of Paducah), and Bill Monroe appear at a WWII bond drive.

In 2007, the Opry teamed up with the US Postal Service and the US Department of Defense's program America Supports You to send the "World's Largest Care Package" to troops overseas.

WORLD'S LARGEST CARE PACKAGE

It's a wacky world as described by the comedy greats who have been members of the Grand Ole Opry over the years. Storytellers like Minnie Pearl, Rod Brasfield, and Jerry Clower regaled audiences with hilarious tales about the goings-on of the characters in their rural Southern hometowns. Musical comedians such as Lonzo and Oscar, Grandpa Jones, and Stringbean created unforgettable characters and paired great pickin' with humorous songs and on-stage antics.

Many of the Opry's comedy stars also appeared as regulars on the syndicated television series *Hee Haw*, which was taped at the Opry House in Studio A for many years. Mike Snider, a graduate of *Hee Haw*, carries on the tradition as a member of the Opry today. His mix of jokes, string band music, and unexpected banter with announcers and his co-stars keeps the audience in stitches—and in awe of his banjo skills.

"I'm goin' back to the wagon, boys, these shoes are killin' me."

-*THE DUKE OF PADUCAH*

Buck Owens and Roy Clark in the *Hee Haw* cornfield, 1979

Hee Haw's Culhanes, L to R: Gordie Tapp, Junior Samples, Grandpa Jones, and Lulu Roman, 1972

"Rindercella slopped her dripper."

-ARCHIE CAMPBELL

The décor is a laugh-riot of color in dressing room #6. Warm yellow walls set off the colorful custom-designed sofa covered in red, green, and purple velvet. Two roomy slipper chairs sport multi-colored cloverleaf upholstery that pops off the striped carpet. Bright fiberglass garden stools provide extra seating and serve as end tables. For one more fun-filled touch, framed photos of the Opry's all-time comedy greats stretch out over the sofa in the pattern of a big, wide smile.

"I'm my own Grandpa..."

-LONZO AND OSCAR

Ferlin Husky's comedic alter ego, Simon Crum, takes over during a 1956 Friday Night Frolic show.

Lonzo and Oscar clown on the Grand Ole Opry, 1954

This 1960 photo demonstrates why Stringbean's outfit had the audience laughing before he said a word.

Roy Acuff laughs as Jerry Clower tells one of his stories, during Clower's 1974 Opry induction.

Family band The Whites have been Opry members since 1984.
L to R: Cheryl, Buck, Rosie, and Sharon.

The Opry is a great place to come home to for artists who spend so much of their time traveling. But, over the years, the Grand Ole Opry has occasionally picked up and hit the road, taking its one-of-a-kind show to the fans on their home turf.

The first known Opry road show was in the early 1930s at a Fourth of July picnic in West Tennessee. After that, tent shows managed by Roy Acuff, Bill Monroe, and others blanketed the country, and tours of military bases in the US and abroad followed. There have been historic shows at Carnegie Hall in 1947, 1961, and 2005. Nationwide tours with a full roster of Opry talent were launched in 1991 with the Grand Ole Opry True Value American Tour and the Opry's Great American Road Show in 2004 and 2005. After the May 2010 flood temporarily forced the show out of the Grand Ole Opry House, the Opry undertook what was wryly called the "High Water Tour," performing at several different Nashville venues while the flood damage was repaired.

Opry members Minnie Pearl, Grandpa Jones, Faron Young, Patsy Cline, and Bill Monroe receive the key to New York City during their 1961 visit for a benefit show at Carnegie Hall.

The cast of 2005's *Grand Ole Opry at Carnegie Hall* takes the stage for the finale.

The décor of dressing room #7 is an exotic mix of pieces that have been gathered from across the globe. A tiger-printed cowhide draped over the sofa, an Indian rug, and gold-colored steamer trunk end tables are a few highlights. Photos and posters from Grand Ole Opry road shows fill the walls.

The Grand Ole Opry troupe of the Camel Caravan (1941–42), which toured US Army bases in the states and the Panama Canal Zone, included Minnie Pearl, Pee Wee King, and Eddy Arnold.

80th ANNIVERSARY CELEBRATION
GRAND OLE OPRY
AT
CARNEGIE HALL

Vince Gill • Brad Paisley
Jimmy Dickens • Trace Adkins
Trisha Yearwood • Alan Jackson
Charley Pride • Alison Krauss
Bill Anderson • Martina McBride
Ricky Skaggs

NOVEMBER 14, 2005
8:00 PM

© 2005 Hatch Show Print

Poster for the Opry's 2005 Carnegie Hall show

A poster at Carnegie Hall advertised the first Grand Ole Opry show there in 1947. Ernest Tubb, Minnie Pearl, and George D. Hay were on the bill.

The cast for the Great American Road Show, 2004

Fans line up to attend a Grand Ole Opry tent show in Mobile, Alabama, in the early 1940s.

Dinah Shore (center) poses with bandleader Beasley Smith and WSM staffer Marge Cooney in the 1940s.

Though the Grand Ole Opry has been broadcast from many places, WSM has been its radio home since the first Saturday night it hit the air. Conceived by company executive Edwin Craig as a service of the National Life and Accident Insurance Company, the station (with call letters taken from the company motto "We Shield Millions") launched on October 5, 1925, to great fanfare and with absolutely no country music on the schedule. This changed quickly when the station hired George D. Hay as its director, and he soon had local old-time musicians performing a barn dance show (later named the Grand Ole Opry) every Saturday night.

1932 was a momentous year for WSM. Engineer Jack Dewitt oversaw the construction of a new 878-foot, diamond-shaped, 50,000-watt transmission tower—then the tallest in the country—which broadcast WSM across the United States and into Canada. The new tower inspired the station's nickname, "Air Castle of the South."

Along with the Grand Ole Opry, WSM produced many other world-class programs during its early days. *Magnolia Blossoms*, featuring gospel music from Fisk University singers, and a pop music program called *Sunday Down South* were both picked up by the NBC

A classic WSM studio mic from the 1940s

network. Named *Radio and Records* magazine's "Country Radio Station of the Century" in 2000, WSM surprisingly did not have an all-country format until the late 1970s.

WSM has boasted incredible talent through the years, including Snooky Lanson, Dinah Shore, Pat Sajak, and Ralph Emery. Behind the scenes, it was WSM employees who created the foundations of the country music industry. The first country music publishing company, the first artist management agency, the first booking agency, and the first recording studio in Nashville were all created by WSM employees. Nashville's first million-selling record was recorded in WSM Studio C, and it was WSM announcer David Cobb who coined Nashville's moniker "Music City USA." The tradition of excellence continues today with current WSM and Opry announcers Bill Cody and Eddie Stubbs having been elected to the Country Radio Hall of Fame.

The Air Castle dressing room recalls the days when the station was located in the plush National Life headquarters in downtown Nashville. Well-worn leather club chairs and dark wood complement photographs depicting important figures and events in WSM's history.

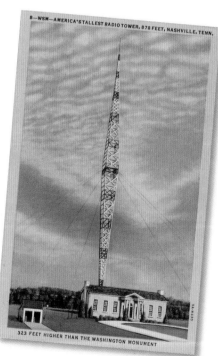

A 1930s postcard featuring the WSM tower

WSM disk jockey Ralph Emery welcomes Connie Smith to the studio in 1969. Emery hosted an influential late night country music show on WSM and is a member of the Radio, Country Music, and Country Radio Halls of Fame.

WSM engineer Jack Dewitt (L) and founder Edwin Craig (R) meet at the National Life offices in 1947.

Noontime Neighbors goes on the air from WSM Studio C, c. 1945.

"The first time we played the Opry at the Grand Ole Opry House they let us use the 'It Takes Two' dressing room. Just walking in and seeing photos of Johnny and June, Porter and Dolly, and Loretta and Conway was a very 'oh my gosh, we're playing the Grand Ole Opry' moment." – Shawna Thompson, Thompson Square.

Where would the "Louisiana Woman" be without her "Mississippi Man"? What if that "Golden Ring" with just one tiny little stone stayed in the pawn shop in Chicago? And who would have made sure Johnny combed his hair before going to "Jackson"? Two heads are better than one, and there are two sides to every story, so it's no wonder that some of the most fun and intriguing country music has come in the form of a duet. The It Takes Two dressing room salutes a category of country that's hotter than a pepper sprout—the duo.

The first time Johnny Cash and June Carter met was backstage at the Opry. He told her he was going to marry her someday. She laughed.

"Ever since I was a little girl, I've always wanted to do what Dolly, Tammy, and Loretta did," says Kellie Pickler. "I've wanted to put my life in a song." Pickler says she loves the duets those three did with the likes of Porter Wagoner, George Jones, and Conway Twitty. "I love to go online and watch those songs," she shares. "You can see the chemistry between them." Pickler reprised one of her favorite duets, "Jackson," by Johnny and June Carter Cash, on the Opry stage with Ronnie Milsap in 2012.

The Opry has spotlighted some of the greatest duos in country music. Married couples such as Wilma Lee and Stoney Cooper, Curly Fox and Texas Ruby, and Vince Gill and Amy Grant have made the music business a family affair. Other duos have doubled-up on the talents of stars like Porter Wagoner and Dolly Parton, Jack Greene and Jeannie Seely, or Conway Twitty and Loretta Lynn to create a sum even greater than its parts.

Because the 1960s were a golden age for country duets, that era is the inspiration for dressing room #9. Chocolate brown walls contrast with furnishings in aqua blue, cream, and gold. The low-slung couch is covered with cream vinyl and aqua velvet and topped with decidedly mod print pillows. Two often-coveted turquoise and gold pottery lamps are reminiscent of an *I Dream of Jeannie* bottle, and of course there is a cream-colored shag rug on the floor to pull the 60s vibe together.

Loretta Lynn recorded three albums of duets with the great Ernest Tubb before forming her musical partnership with Conway Twitty.

Jim Ed Brown and Helen Cornelius recorded a string of thirteen Top-40 hits between 1976 and 1981, including the #1 smash, "I Don't Want to Have to Marry You."

George Jones and Tammy Wynette's marriage lasted fewer than seven years, but the music they made together will last for generations.

Blake Shelton and Miranda Lambert met singing a duet, and won the 2012 CMA Song of the Year award for "Over You," a song they wrote together.

The Grand Ole Opry loves having company. Some of the folks who have stopped by to say hello, take a bow, and even pick or sing a number or two might be surprising. The Friends & Neighbors dressing room is dedicated to some of the Opry's country (and city) cousins who have visited over the years. The guest list is a who's who in the fields of entertainment, journalism, politics, and art, and the collection of photographs on the walls gives a glimpse of the variety of visitors over the years.

Comedians Bob Hope and George Burns have appeared. Governor-turned senator Lamar Alexander of Tennessee and Senator Robert Byrd of West Virginia each played on the Grand Ole Opry (the former on piano and the latter on fiddle). Paul and Linda McCartney stopped in with kids and

After his 2011 Opry performance sitting in on bass with Luke Bryan, Lester Holt joked, "I'm only doing the news because I can't seem to make it as a successful musician, so in the meantime, I read the news. When my album gets done, then I'm outta here!"

Paul McCartney and family visit with Dolly Parton and Porter Wagoner in 1974. His song "Sally G" was inspired by his Opryland visit, where he heard the fiddle tune, "Sally Goodin."

"It was such a special evening . . . being there at the hallowed Grand Ole Opry!"

"I have had an opportunity in my life to be in significant places. I pitched a so-called perfect game in Yankee Stadium. I got a chance to ride with the buffalo—something people haven't done for 200 years, and I stand at this stage and I look out, and I think about the people who have been here, you know, and I am humbled by this." – Kevin Costner, 2008

balloons in tow after a day at Opryland theme park. Artist Andy Warhol attended the show and visited backstage. Young Anderson Cooper (age 8) can be seen posing with his mother, Gloria Vanderbilt, and family. Actor/musicians Jack Black, Kevin Bacon, and Kevin Costner have taken their turns on the Opry stage. CBS's Charles Osgood and Bob Schieffer (p. 80) have each performed on the Opry as well. *Good Morning America* anchor Robin Roberts has taken over hosting duties on two occasions for the annual "Opry Goes Pink" show that serves to raise funds for the fight against breast cancer.

The eclectic mix of guests speaks volumes about the universal appeal of the Opry, and reflects the mantra of all good Southern hosts, "Y'all come!"

Basketball icons the Harlem Globetrotters paid a visit to the Opry on October 19, 2010, delighting the audience with their legendary ball-handling skills while the Opry band played their theme song, "Sweet Georgia Brown." Here, Little Jimmy Dickens, who lettered in basketball in high school, gets into the act.

"I think I've got some hillbilly in my roots." – Jack Black, 2009

Ernest Tubb chats with music legend Tony Bennett backstage at an Opry television taping in 1955. Bennett made a guest appearance singing Hank Williams' "Cold, Cold Heart," which he took to the top of the pop charts in 1951.

"JUST GO OUT THERE AND HAVE FUN" ~ MY NIGHT AT THE OPRY

By CBS Chief Washington Correspondent and moderator of Face The Nation *Bob Schieffer*

Brad Paisley shares the stage with news legend Bob Schieffer, October 10, 2008.

In 2007, Bill Geist of CBS Sunday Morning shared the story of Honky Tonk Confidential, a band fronted by the Emmy Award-winning dean of political news, CBS's Bob Schieffer, making its debut in the city that never sleeps. At the end of the piece, Schieffer declared, "We're really excited, you know this engagement here in New York, I mean you know, you come to New York this is it," he said. "If you can make it here, I think we're one step closer to the Grand Ole Opry." Opry staffers took note, and a little over a year later, the newsman realized his goal, performing during a special Opry show arranged in conjunction with the 2008 presidential debate hosted by Nashville's Belmont University. Schieffer shares his impressions of his Opry debut, and of sharing the stage with some of the Opry's biggest stars.

I'll never forget my night at the Opry. We had been invited to perform the weekend that Belmont University was hosting the 2008 presidential debate and it was the weekend before I was moderating the final debate at Hofstra University. It was the first time I had been to Nashville since my college days when some classmates and I drove up from Fort Worth to see the Opry. We saw Ernest Tubb that night and Cousin Minnie Pearl. I couldn't believe I was standing in the same place they had stood.

Backstage, I was plenty nervous. But Trisha Yearwood told me, "Just go out there and have fun." Easy for her to say, but not for me since I followed her on the program.

As it turned out, there were a lot of reporters in the audience and they gave us a big welcome and we actually got a standing ovation as we left.

Brad Paisley and his band followed us and Brad said, "Thanks for coming folks, I'm not following that." Of course, he did, and he called me and our back-up singers out to the stage and asked us to join in his closing song "Alcohol." Since then Brad and I have become good friends and I get back to Nashville every so often—like every struggling young songwriter, I keep hoping someone will cut one of my songs.

People asked what surprised me about that night and it had to be just how nice everybody there treated us—not just Brad and Trisha, but Darius Rucker, Josh Turner, and all the Opry folk.

The other question people ask: "Did being on *Face the Nation* prepare you for the Opry?" The answer is no—nothing really prepares you for walking on the stage that is still alive with the spirit of all the country greats. But I also tell them this: the Opry prepared me for the presidential debate the next weekend. After you've stood on that Opry stage, nothing really scares you and for sure, nothing could be more fun.

⋮ Bob Schieffer ⋮

ON THE OPRY FRIDAY NIGHT, BACK ON CBS BY 'SUNDAY MORNING'

Bob Schieffer's Opry visit in 2008 was influential in another newsman's visit two years later. Radio Hall of Fame member and host of *CBS Sunday Morning* Charles Osgood made an appearance as Opry guest announcer and also took to the piano to lead the Opry audience in "You Are My Sunshine" during the Opry's 85th Birthday Bash on October 8, 2010. In the Friends And Neighbors dressing room backstage, Osgood said, "Most of all, I've been jealous—eating my heart out—about the fact that Bob Schieffer was already on the Grand Ole Opry, and I just can't wait to get back to New York and let him know on Sunday morning what I did over the weekend!"

⋮ Charles Osgood ⋮

When Marty Stuart surprised Dierks Bentley with an invitation to join the Opry, he jokingly asked, "Will you marry the Grand Ole Opry?" There was certainly a seed of truth in Stuart's joke, because to become a member of the Opry is to join a family. It's a great big family with an amazing family tree, and this clan just so happens to have a reunion backstage every week.

The Welcome to the Family dressing room is a celebration of the rituals of Opry membership. First comes the invitation—a closely-guarded secret orchestrated to surprise the invitee. For Bentley, this meant having a concert in Los Angeles interrupted by Stuart's proposal. Darius Rucker kindly agreed to take a few questions from Opry audience members, never expecting Brad Paisley to pop up and ask him to join the family. And Blake Shelton was the first member to get the invite through a tweet. After the initial surprise, the answer was—"YES!"

On induction night, friends and family crowd in backstage to celebrate the new member in song, in words, and in cake! Each new member is

Brad Paisley receives a Christmas gift to remember when Santa (Little Jimmy Dickens) and Mrs. Claus (Jeannie Seely) pay a special visit alongside Bill Anderson to invite him to be a member of the Opry on December 16, 2000.

Loretta Lynn, pictured here in 1962, jumps for joy when Opry manager Ott Devine asks her to join the Opry cast.

presented with the Opry Member Award, a bronze statuette that is a replica of the Opry microphone stand on a circular base made of wood from the original pews preserved during the restoration of Ryman Auditorium. It's the physical symbol of membership, but the real reward is intangible, and much more valuable—it's knowing that one is a part of country music's most illustrious family.

"Tonight for me is the Nashville dream. Tonight is the pinnacle . . . this is the reason that you move to Nashville. If you're me, this is what I wanted from the beginning . . . to make a mark in country music. This is the ultimate one, I think."

– Blake Shelton on the night of his Opry induction

"The ultimate dream when you're in country music is to be asked to join the Grand Ole Opry. It's the cornerstone of country music. I don't know if Nashville or country music would exist if it wasn't for this foundation, and I'm proud to be a part of it."

– Alan Jackson

"I think the importance of being a member of the Grand Ole Opry is to have deep respect for the music that came before, and to feel the responsibility of making sure country music is honored for generations to come. It's an elite group to get to belong to, and once you're invited into those loving arms, you're always family. What a great gift!"

– Trisha Yearwood

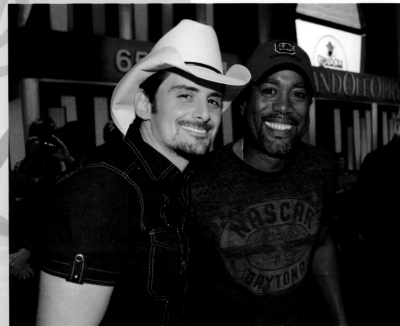

Brad Paisley poses with Darius Rucker backstage on October 2, 2012, after surprising Rucker with an invitation to join the Opry family.

Marty Stuart "pops the question" to Dierks Bentley about joining the Opry cast during Bentley's Los Angeles concert on July 6, 2005.

Trisha Yearwood says half the fun of a night at the Grand Ole Opry is spending time in the Glitz and Glamour room. Not unlike the goings-on in beauty parlors and powder rooms anywhere else in the world, the Glitz and Glamour room offers the best spot for "girl talk" anywhere backstage.

"Sitting backstage in the 'girls' make-up room is one of the best places to hang out," Yearwood says. "You learn so much, from what it was like in the early days, traveling the country in cars, to recipe tips from Jeanne Pruett. All the gals, especially Pruett, Jeannie Seely, Jean Shepard, and Connie Smith, have always made me feel like one of the girls. And it's an amazing 'club' to belong to!"

Dolly Parton, who, along with Loretta Lynn, says the motto for Opry female hairdos used to be "let us spray!" once recalled how a very young Patty Loveless used to hang around her at the Opry "and ask me for hints for make-up. But thank the Lord she didn't take 'em!"

Opry members Lorrie Morgan and Pam Tillis have been members of "the club" for decades, each the daughter of a Country Music Hall of Famer (George Morgan and Mel Tillis, respectively) and each having made her Opry debut on the stage of Ryman Auditorium before she was old enough to get a driver's license. That's a lot of years backstage to soak up glamour on display by the likes of Dottie West, Tammy Wynette, Barbara Mandrell, and others first-hand. With more than 30 Top 10-hits between them, the pair has performed dozens of shows together across the country as the "Grits & Glamour" tour.

Barbara Mandrell gets glamorous with the help of makeup artist Elizabeth Linneman, 1981.

BACKSTAGE ENCOUNTERS
of THE Glitzy and Glamorous

Loretta Lynn

Carrie Underwood

Whether it be in make-up chairs in the Glitz and Glamour room or passing in hallways, dozens of queens of country music have met for the first time backstage at the Opry. No two backstage encounters are ever the same, as evidenced by stories from Jan Howard, an Opry member since 1971, and Carrie Underwood, who joined the family in 2008.

Carrie Underwood meets Loretta Lynn

(as told by Carrie Underwood)

I've always been a fan of Loretta Lynn. She really is someone for all of us ladies to love and look up to! So, imagine how happy I was when I found out she was going to be at the Opry on the same night as me! I got ready and was hanging out backstage talking to some friends when someone came up behind me and smacked me on the rear end! For a split second, I was actually kind of shocked that someone would ever smack me on the bum like that, but when I turned around and realized it was Loretta, I just had to laugh! I love it that that was my very first time meeting Loretta. That's just how she is! No one is a stranger . . .

Jan Howard meets Patsy Cline

(as told by Jan Howard)

I have loved Patsy Cline's music since I first heard her voice, long before I started singing. But when I came to Nashville, Johnny Cash gave me a bit of advice when it came to playing the Opry: "Just do your song and leave . . . that way you won't get into trouble." I had no idea what trouble he meant, but I did just that. I was afraid to just walk up and introduce myself to an Opry star, afraid they'd say "Who?" so I didn't. A lot of people took it as being conceited, but I was honored to be there and just very green.

But if Patsy was on the show, I'd wait until she sang before I'd leave. One night after she sang, I was in the dressing room (which was the ladies' restroom) changing clothes, when the door burst open, and there stood Patsy in that red and white cowgirl outfit, hands on her hips, and "attitude" written all over her face.

"Well," she said, "you're a conceited little son of a bitch." I was shocked, to say the least. She went on, "You just come in here, do your bit, and leave. You don't say hello, kiss my ass, or anything."

That did it. I stood up, faced her, and said, "Wait just a damned minute. Where I came from, it's the people there who make a stranger feel welcome, and not a damned one here has made me feel welcome, and that includes you." She just looked at me for a minute then laughed her booming laugh and said, "You're alright, honey. Anybody that'll stand up to the Cline is alright. We're gonna be good friends."

And, for the short time that was to be the rest of her life, we were.

A bevy of Opry beauties pose backstage, October 7, 1961. L to R: Minnie Pearl, Wilma Lee Cooper, Jan Howard, Skeeter Davis, June Carter, and Kitty Wells.

Patsy Cline

Jan Howard

"'Honky Tonk Angels' is my favorite dressing room, for sure. The photos are my favorite part. I like to look into all their gorgeous faces and then can't believe I get to be in that room and work where they work." – Elizabeth Cook

This one's for the girls. For the little girls who grew up dreaming of the glamorous life of a country music star—and for the young women who, even after discovering that the life of a performer is hard, hard work, stuck with it and triumphed.

Dressing room #14 is named Honky Tonk Angels after Kitty Wells' 1952 #1 hit, "It Wasn't God Who Made Honky Tonk Angels," an answer song to Hank Thompson's recording of "Wild Side of Life," and the first chart-topper by a female country artist. Thompson's song bemoaned a woman who preferred the nightlife to home life, and Wells recorded a direct response from the female perspective, arguing, "It wasn't God who made honky tonk angels as you said in the words of your song. Too many times married men think they're still single. That has caused many a good girl to go wrong." It may seem tame today, but in 1952, Wells' song was scandalous and banned from many radio stations. But the recording was a watershed moment, and women have been singing their side of the story ever since.

Emmylou Harris, 2007

Pam Tillis, performing here in 2006, learned from the legends, growing up amongst Nashville music royalty.

"When we crossed the Canadian border into the United States, the guard at the border said, 'Where are y'all headed?' And we said, 'The Grand Ole Opry!'"

Before that time, conventional wisdom held that women could never succeed as solo acts in country music. Pioneering artists including Kitty Wells and Jean Shepard proved that belief wrong, and following generations of women, including Loretta Lynn, Dolly Parton, and Reba McEntire, have conquered not only music but every form of entertainment—from publishing to film, to television, to Broadway.

The décor in dressing room #14 reflects the class and sass of the Opry's honky tonk angels, who are depicted in photographs covering the walls. Shimmering champagne-colored wall covering sets off the focal points of the room—a funky curved chaise-style sofa covered with platinum metallic faux ostrich skin and a leopard print rug—because let's face it, every so often, a honky tonk angel needs to get back to the wild side of life.

Patsy Cline, 1962

The Queen of Country Music, Kitty Wells, performs on the Opry, 1958.

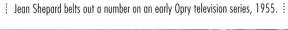
Jean Shepard belts out a number on an early Opry television series, 1955.

Reba McEntire, 2009

DRESSING ROOM 15

Riders In The Sky are: Joey the CowPolka King, Woody Paul, Ranger Doug, and Too Slim.

No other American character has captured the imagination as enduringly as the cowboy. The white-hatted hero of dime novels, campfire songs, and "B" movies found his (and her) way into country music from the very start, and shows no sign of hitting the trail anytime soon.

The first Opry member to embrace the cowboy image was singer/songwriter/actor Zeke Clements, who billed himself as the Dixie Yodeler. The Opry's first cowgirl hit the stage in 1937. Texas Ruby Owens grew up singing to the cowhands on her father's Texas ranch and joined the Opry with her fiddling husband, Curly Fox.

Marty Robbins, pictured here in the 1950s, loved the lore of the West and authentic cowboy ballads. His masterpiece, "El Paso," has gone on to be a classic in its own right.

Singing cowboy film star Tex Ritter sang the Oscar-winning theme to the movie *High Noon* in 1952. Pictured here on a 1960s television appearance, his repertoire included many authentic turn-of-the-century cowboy songs.

No Opry act has done more to keep the sounds and romance of Western music alive as "America's Favorite Cowboys," Riders In The Sky. Since 1977, the group has been honoring the musical tradition of the likes of Sons of the Pioneers, Gene Autry, and Tex Ritter. But, Ranger Doug, Woody Paul, Too Slim, and Joey the CowPolka King are no museum piece. They have added dozens of contemporary compositions to the Western music repertoire, starred in their own radio and television series, and introduced new generations to cowboy cool through their Grammy-winning music for the Pixar films *Toy Story 2* and *Monsters, Inc.* Since 1982, they have been comporting themselves in "The Cowboy Way" as members of the Opry cast.

Dressing room #15 is inspired by the lore of cowboys and the West. A pair of Hollywood-worthy distressed leather and chrome chairs sit on the weathered bunkhouse-style floor, and the red dressing screen is a dead ringer for a saloon's swingin' doors. A pair of mounted longhorns crowns the mirror, and it is all tied together by a striped wool rug as pretty as an Arizona sunset.

Zeke Clements temporarily left Nashville for a career in Hollywood, where he voiced the character of Dopey in Walt Disney's *Snow White and the Seven Dwarfs*. Here he performs on WSM in 1944.

Pee Wee King and his Golden West Cowboys, pictured here c. 1938, dazzled audiences with their cowboy duds and polished Western swing music. L to R: Pee Wee King, Abner Sims, Texas Daisy, Jack Skaggs, Milton Estes, and Curley Rhodes.

Pee Wee King's hand-tooled leather boots

"King of the Cowboys," Roy Rogers is met at the Nashville airport by young fans in 1957.

Cousin Minnie

"How-dee! I'm just so proud to be here!"

Cousin Minnie Pearl's greeting rang out from the Opry stage for over 50 years, welcoming the audience and making them proud to be wherever Minnie was.

Born Sarah Ophelia Colley in Centerville, Tennessee, young "Ophie," as she was called, grew up aspiring to be a great dramatic actress. "I dreamed of seeing my name in lights on Broadway. I dreamed of following in the trail of Katharine Hepburn and other great actresses." she mused. But her natural comedic talents always shone through. Though she was educated at Nashville's prestigious Ward-Belmont School, she developed a naïve, gregarious country girl character, which in 1940, took her to the Grand Ole Opry where audiences fell in love.

Minnie was famous for the warmth and kindness she showed to newcomers waiting nervously in the wings to take the Opry stage. From Hank Williams to Johnny Cash to Barbara Mandrell, Minnie's welcome soothed their nerves, and her ongoing friendship was unwavering in the best and the worst of times.

Minnie and her fellers, Bill Carlisle, Grandpa Jones, security guard Mr. Norris, Ray Price, Carl Smith, and Smilin' Eddie Hill, congregate backstage in 1954.

These well-worn Mary Jane shoes were part of Minnie's costume for over 40 years.

Minnie Pearl and Rod Brasfield formed a hilarious comedy duo for ten years beginning in 1948. She recalled, "I had some of my happiest times on radio working with him every Saturday night." Here they perform their "double comedy" (no straight man) routines on the Opry in 1954.

After marrying the love of her life, Henry Cannon, Sarah Cannon became active in countless charities, donating her time and talents, and gaining acceptance for country music entertainers in Nashville's social circles—something that had long been denied.

Dressing room #16 is specially designed both to honor Minnie Pearl and to welcome guests with the same warm hospitality she extended to everyone she met. The décor is a blend of the Southern charm and whimsy that characterize Minnie and her creator, Sarah Cannon. Weathered wood recalls the thousands of stages trod by those famous Mary Jane shoes. The overstuffed sofa, wing chairs, and palette of aqua, gold, and salmon pink would be perfectly at home in any proper parlor. A collection of framed photographs are lit by a unique floral light fixture inspired by Minnie's hat—all it needs is a $1.98 price tag!

With Roy Acuff, 1975

Minnie celebrates her 50th anniversary as an Opry member in 1991. Behind her are 50 dozen roses Dwight Yoakam sent her for the occasion.

With Hank Williams, 1950

Sarah Cannon works on Minnie's hat, c. 1950.

The great songwriter Harlan Howard described country music as "three chords and the truth." That definition, like the best country songs, is deceptively simple. But Nashville *is* first and foremost a songwriter's town, and as the name of the dressing room says, it all begins with a song. Some of country music's finest writers have introduced their future classics on the Opry stage or found the perfect artist to cut a song backstage.

His Opry contemporaries often recalled how the great Hank Williams, whose songwriting earned him the moniker "The Hillbilly Shakespeare," would pitch new songs backstage to other artists, and then after receiving praise, decide he should cut the song himself. Jimmy Dickens was offered and wanted to record, "Hey Good Lookin'," but Williams proceeded to record it after all, jokingly telling Dickens, "It's too good a song for you anyway."

It was a marathon session of listening to Hank Williams recordings that inspired Josh Turner to write his song, "Long Black Train," which he introduced to a standing ovation on the Opry in 2001. Turner later found a duet partner for another of his songs backstage. He played "Me and God," for Dr. Ralph Stanley backstage at the Opry one night, and asked the bluegrass legend to record the song with him. It went on to be nominated for Vocal Event of the Year at the 2007 ACM Awards.

The Louvin Brothers, Ira (L) and Charlie (R), wrote nearly 200 country and gospel songs together.

Many visitors don't recognize Willie Nelson's photo from his Grand Ole Opry days in the early 1960s, but they certainly recognize his songs from that era, including "Night Life," "Funny How Time Slips Away," and "Crazy."

Songwriting master Bill Anderson has seen his compositions reach the country charts for six straight decades. In addition to his own recordings, greats such as Ray Price, Lefty Frizzell, Connie Smith, and George Strait have taken Anderson's songs to #1.

Even the most venerated songwriters never stop looking for a hit. Former Opry announcer Keith Bilbrey recounted the story of the night Bill Monroe asked Bilbrey to take him to Vince Gill's dressing room. Monroe played a song for Gill all the way through, enlisting Gill's band for accompaniment, and then urged the young star when he finished, "You ought to record that song, boy. It would be a powerful number for you to do and folks all over the world would love you for it." Gill was rendered speechless, having been personally pitched a song by the Father of Bluegrass backstage at the Grand Ole Opry!

A sleek black leather sofa and contemporary wingback chairs give dressing room #17 the sophisticated air of a Music City publishing house, but it is comfortable enough to kick back and work out a verse or two and a chorus. The walls feature photographs of all the inductees to the Nashville Songwriter's Hall of Fame who have also been members of the Grand Ole Opry.

Some of country's most enduring songs have come from the pens of Opry members.

Mel Tillis has written hit songs for himself and countless others, acted in feature films, and is a member of the Country Music Hall of Fame.

Hank Williams, "The Hillbilly Shakespeare," still casts a long shadow on country songwriting today.

Dolly Parton has said, "I feel like anybody can sing, but not everybody can write. My songs tell how I feel. I get more out of writing than singing."

An international icon, Johnny Cash's music is as popular today as it has ever been.

"I love the 'Women of Country' dressing room, naturally. My picture is hanging next to many of my idols. Plus, it's such a beautiful room!"
– Carrie Underwood

"I'm on the same wall as Dolly Parton and that makes me happy!"
– Pam Tillis

The Women of Country dressing room is, not surprisingly, a favorite among the female Opry performers, and not only due to the elegant décor. Knowing that they are occupying the same dressing room that their idols use, and seeing their photographs placed alongside the legendary ladies of country means the world to the artists following in the footsteps of the all-time greats. The glamorous room is in many ways a shrine to the special sisterhood shared by those women who have chosen the not-always-glamorous life of making music.

Ashley Monroe and Emmylou Harris, 2006

Two women in country who prove that big voices can come in small packages: Connie Smith and Martina McBride backstage, circa 1994

Carrie Underwood and Barbara Mandrell: an American Idol meets one of her idols backstage in 2006.

Reba McEntire, Loretta Lynn, and Patty Loveless backstage on January 15, 2000

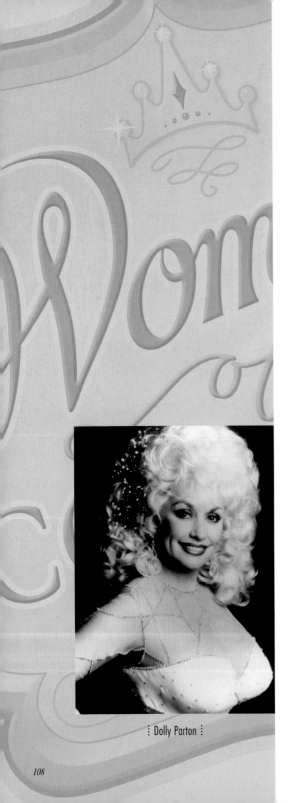

A plush dressing room is a rarity on the road, and even at the Opry, the facilities have not always been quite so comfortable. Women who performed on the Opry during its time at Ryman Auditorium reminisce about the then-cramped backstage area of the Ryman, where the male performers had two rooms in which to dress, rehearse, and converse, while the women were relegated to the small ladies' restroom. With a wry nostalgia, Barbara Mandrell recalls those days: "What I remember most . . . is dressing and getting made up in the toilet, which was the women's dressing room. That was really close, and warm and friendly sharing that crowded space with Loretta Lynn and Connie Smith and Dolly Parton and Jeannie Seely."

Today, there are beautiful dressing rooms a-plenty, and Mandrell, along with all of her former roommates, are featured in classic black and white publicity photos decorating the walls of the Women of Country dressing room. The photos, along with the shimmering antique gold walls and rich powder blue furnishings, give the room an old Hollywood vibe that can make anyone feel like a movie star—or a queen of country music.

Dolly Parton

Dottie West

Barbara Mandrell

Jeannie Seely

Martina McBride

Renaissance man Marty Stuart designed Wagonmaster in honor of one of his personal heroes, Porter Wagoner.

"I love Marty Stuart's dressing room. I love how he has used design to connect the legends of the Grand Ole Opry. I believe Marty is one of our treasures in country music. He respects our history, how we got here, and where we are going next." – Duane Allen, Oak Ridge Boys

Singer, songwriter, mandolin player, historian, guitarist, photographer, producer, television star, curator, designer, lifelong student, and passionate teacher—Opry member Marty Stuart is all these things and more. He first hit the Opry stage at age 13 as a guest of Lester Flatt. He remembers, "When the song was finished the crowd kept applauding. I got scared and thought I'd done something wrong. I looked at Lester and said, 'What do I do?' He started laughing and said, 'Do it again.'"

Performing on Porter Wagoner's 50th Opry anniversary show, May 19, 2007

One of Porter Wagoner's signature rhinestone jackets

Stuart produced Wagoner's final album, *Wagonmaster*. The song "Eleven Cent Cotton" is a depression-era song that the two reimagined for the album.

The prodigious start in the music business may have seemed a tough act to follow, but stints touring with Bob Dylan and Johnny Cash, a chart-topping solo career, a beloved television show, and position of respected country music expert and revered statesman prove that the encore with Lester Flatt was not beginner's luck!

Dressing room #19, which for years was used by Porter Wagoner, displays another of Stuart's artistic talents. Named Wagonmaster for his friend and mentor who led a band of that name, the room was personally designed by Stuart as a tribute to the "sparkle and twang" for which both he and Wagoner are known. Wagoner was a member of the Grand Ole Opry for over 50 years, the host of a pioneering country music television series, a celebrated songwriter, singer, producer, and a member of the Country Music Hall of Fame.

The lush red and purple décor in the room is surrounded by photographs and memorabilia from Stuart's and Wagoner's careers. A display case full of glittering artifacts from Stuart's personal collection casts a lively sparkle throughout the room.

Nothing says country music like rhinestones! Stuart has filled a display case in the dressing room with treasures from his personal collection.

Porter and Marty, 2009

Marty Stuart takes a mandolin solo while performing with Lester Flatt and the Nashville Grass, October 1973.

FAMILY ROOM

Theories abound, but there is no verifiable origin of the term "Green Room." Technically, it is a room close to the stage where performers and guests can relax. At the Grand Ole Opry, no one worries about the origin of the name. In fact, the Opry just calls it the Family Room, and as the name attests, it is a perfect spot for lounging and visiting with family and friends.

The walls are an Opry family album—covered with photographs of cherished special occasions and great moments. Comfortable furniture is arranged in conversation groupings—an invitation to sit a spell. On show nights, Opry stars and other backstage guests mingle over coffee or lemonade, chat, pose for photos, sign autographs, and, of course, keep an eye on the television monitor where the show onstage is broadcast—just to make sure they aren't late for their segment!

One piece of the décor that many people miss unless it is pointed out is a 17-foot-long decorative strip of hammered iron attached along the east wall in the Family Room at 46 inches high, the height reached by flood waters in the room on May 2, 2010. Created by metal artist Andrew Ferrin, it is a subtle historical marker, but a powerful reminder of what can be accomplished through the hard work, passion, and perseverance that has been the hallmark of the artists and staff of the Grand Ole Opry—not only in recovering from a 500-year flood, but throughout the history of country music's most enduring icon.

Charlie Daniels cuts his 75th birthday cake in the Opry House Family Room, October 29, 2011.

Backstage guests chat and peruse the photographs lining the walls.

The high water point during the May 2010 flood is represented with this iron marker.

FAMILY ROOM

"I love to look at the pictures on the walls. No matter how many times I've played there and taken in the sights, I always find something new to look at."
– Carrie Underwood

Carrie Underwood is not alone. Backstage visitors love to get caught up in the photos of some of the Opry's most memorable moments and colorful characters. The images on these pages are just a few of those lining the Family Room walls.

Grand Ole Opry founder George D. Hay, "The Solemn Old Judge"

President Ronald Reagan visits the Opry for Roy Acuff's 81st birthday celebration in 1984.

Brad Paisley performs in the East Room of the White House for President Obama and family, July 21, 2009.

The cast of the Grand Ole Opry gathers onstage during the 50th anniversary show in 1975.

Porter Wagoner welcomes James Brown as a guest on the Grand Ole Opry, March 10, 1979.

Garth Brooks presents Carrie Underwood with her Opry Member Award on her induction night, May 10, 2008.

From the annual Grand Ole Opry Duck Hunt, 1974—L to R: Grandpa Jones, Charlie Walker, Stu Phillips, Neil Craig, Jimmy C. Newman, Bud Wendell

A 1934 Opry cast photo taken in WSM's Studio B

ARCHIE CAMPBELL MURAL

With his collection of quick-witted characters, his wacky re-telling of fairy tales such as "Rindercella" and "The Pee Little Thrigs," and the ever-present cigar clenched in his teeth, Archie Campbell had a Vaudeville air about him that was right at home on the set of *Hee Haw* and the stage of the Grand Ole Opry. But the East Tennessee native who began performing to earn money for art supplies was a Renaissance man who wrote and performed comedy and music, hosted a television interview series, and was also a visual artist.

Campbell got his start at Knoxville radio station WNOX in 1936 on *The Mid-Day Merry-Go-Round*, providing comic relief alongside the show's musical star, Roy Acuff. After stints on other East Tennessee stations and service in the Navy during WWII, he eventually landed in Nashville, joined the Grand Ole Opry in 1958, and signed with RCA Records. He recorded comedy albums, sentimental recitations, and a series of country duets with Lorene Mann.

Campbell is best known for his work on *Hee Haw*, where he was a staff writer as well as a star. He created unforgettable characters and skits such as "Doctor Campbell and Nurse Goodbody," "Justus O' Peace," and "The Barber." He also created the famous "Pfft! You Were Gone" bit. Later, he would go on to host the series *Yesteryear in Nashville*, an interview show featuring legends of country music. Campbell passed away in 1987.

Throughout his career in country music and comedy, Archie Campbell continued to paint—mostly regional landscapes, but also portraits and humorous scenes, like the one that serves as the focal point in the Opry House Family Room. The painting was originally created as the cover for the 1966 *Official Opry History-Picture Book* and in 1981, the artwork was enlarged and printed on fabric to create a large mural.

In the painting, Campbell captures the "good-natured riot" that is the Grand Ole Opry. Artists perform onstage, pickers and singers warm up and hang around offstage, square dancers twirl, stage hands move equipment, and fans take photos. Campbell also painted himself into the scene. Behind the announcer's podium on the right side of the painting, in a white and blue-striped jacket and holding a cigar, Campbell depicted himself dancing with a shapely blonde, whom he identified as Dolly Parton—now that's artistic license!

STUDIO A

Studio A is the Grand Ole Opry House's working television studio, where hundreds of scenes and shows appearing on dozens of networks and starring a who's who of country artists and actors have been filmed. The most famed of all shows shot in Studio A was *Hee Haw*, which moved to the studio from downtown Nashville in 1980 and filmed within Studio A's walls through 1991.

The studio space also plays an important role in the life of the Opry family. Because the room is connected to the Opry House, it's the place where the Opry gathers for celebrations of all kinds—to celebrate the show's birthday, to mark a member's milestone Opry anniversary, or maybe to welcome a new member into the fold.

On June 4, 2013, the Opry hosted a welcome home party for frequent guest artist Kellie Pickler to congratulate her on winning season 16 of ABC's *Dancing With the Stars*. Pictured are Kellie and her dance partner, Derek Hough, showing off the cupcakes decorated with a perfect score of "10" that were served at the party.

Diamond Rio performs for and shares career advice with a group of students from Boston's Berklee College of Music in Studio A, March 12, 2011.

The Whites perform "Mansion Over the Hilltop" during the taping of *Opry Legends Gospel Favorites* in Studio A on February 8, 2010.

· YOU ARE INVITED TO CELEBRATE WITH US AS ·

THE GRAND OLE OPRY® WELCOMES

KEITH URBAN

AS ITS NEWEST MEMBER

SATURDAY, APRIL 21, 2012

OPRY HOUSE STUDIO A RECEPTION:
7:00PM - 10:00PM

Including a live feed of the show with
the on-stage induction at approximately 8:30PM.

PLEASE RSVP TO (615) ███-████
BY WEDNESDAY, APRIL 18, 2012.

To purchase tickets to the show, which begins at 7:00PM,
please call Opry VIP Services at ███ ███-████ or
email ████.████@████.███

Please enter through the Opry Backstage parking area and artist entrance.
This invitation is non-transferable.

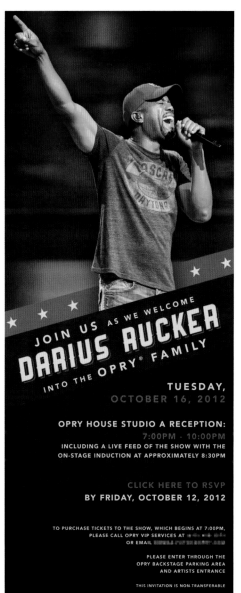

JOIN US AS WE WELCOME

DARIUS RUCKER

INTO THE OPRY® FAMILY

TUESDAY,
OCTOBER 16, 2012

OPRY HOUSE STUDIO A RECEPTION:
7:00PM - 10:00PM
INCLUDING A LIVE FEED OF THE SHOW WITH THE
ON-STAGE INDUCTION AT APPROXIMATELY 8:30PM

CLICK HERE TO RSVP
BY FRIDAY, OCTOBER 12, 2012

TO PURCHASE TICKETS TO THE SHOW, WHICH BEGINS AT 7:00PM,
PLEASE CALL OPRY VIP SERVICES AT ███ ███-████
OR EMAIL ████████ ████@████.███

PLEASE ENTER THROUGH THE
OPRY BACKSTAGE PARKING AREA
AND ARTISTS ENTRANCE

THIS INVITATION IS NON-TRANSFERABLE

Loretta Lynn
CELEBRATING 50 YEARS
WITH THE GRAND OLE OPRY®

Announcing

A show celebrating
Loretta Lynn's 50th Opry Anniversary
September 25, 2012 · 7:00 PM
Grand Ole Opry House

Opry House Studio A Reception

Including a live feed of the show
7:00 PM - 10:00 PM

Please RSVP to (615) 316-6570
by Friday, September 21, 2012

To purchase tickets to the show, please call
Opry VIP Services at (615) 458-3575 or
e-mail donna.futch@opry.com

Please enter through the Opry Backstage parking area and artist entrance.
This invitation is non-transferable.

GRAND OLE OPRY®

HEE HAW: FROM STUDIO  TO THE WORLD

In its more than 20 years on the air during its original run, *Hee Haw* did more than just make people laugh; it made an indelible mark on country music and became, says show host Roy Clark, "an American institution." Created by Canadians Frank Peppiatt and John Aylesworth, the show began as a summer replacement for CBS's *The Smothers Brothers Comedy Hour* on June 15, 1969, moved to first-run syndication after 51 episodes, and became appointment Saturday evening television for fans tuned in across the country. At its height, the program was the nation's #1-rated non-network show, with the residents of Kornfield Kounty reaching 90 percent of US households on 220 television stations.

Hee Haw made stars of cast members such as Junior Samples, Lulu Roman, and the Hager Twins (Jim & Jon). Hosts Roy Clark and Buck Owens, as well as Grandpa Jones and Minnie Pearl, became even bigger stars than the internationally-known talents they were before they paid their first visit to the show's set.

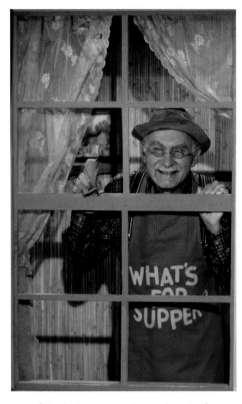

Grandpa Jones answers the eternal question, "What's for supper?" in 1990.

Together with more than 20 other core cast members, the stars brought to life recurring characters such as the Naggers, the Culhanes, and KORN newscaster Charlie Farquharson in beloved locales such as Archie's Barbershop, the General Store, and Samples' famed used car lot. The show's signature cornfield is now rightfully displayed among other country music television artifacts in Nashville's Country Music Hall of Fame and Museum.

Among the countless country superstars who dropped in on the cast for musical numbers as well as the occasional joke were Chet Atkins, Garth Brooks, Reba McEntire, Dolly Parton, Marty Robbins, Ernest Tubb, and Hank Williams Jr. And evidence of *Hee Haw*'s popularity beyond its Southern base are guest appearances by a wide range of celebrities from film, TV, sports, and even Broadway, including Terry Bradshaw, Sammy Davis Jr., and Regis Philbin.

 HUMOR

Lulu Roman: Roy, what letter comes after "A" in the alphabet?

Roy Clark: All of 'em do!

Archie Campbell: I see by the papers up in New York there's a man gets hit by a car every 30 minutes.

Junior Samples: I bet he's getting tired of that by now.

Junior Samples: I hate my mother-in-law.

Gordie Tapp: Well if it wasn't for your mother-in-law, you wouldn't have a wife.

Junior Samples: That's another reason I hate her.

HEE HAW FUN FACTS

NOW THAT'S A LOT OF CORN:

Hee Haw was one of the longest-running syndicated TV shows in history, with 585 episodes produced.

AND THE AWARD GOES TO:

The show won a 1971 Emmy for Outstanding Achievement in Video Tape Editing and received an Entertainers Award at the 2007 TV Land Awards.

THERE THEY GO NAME-DROPPING AGAIN:

Hee Haw continues to be mentioned in mainstream media today, including recent exposure on David Letterman's famed "Top 10 List," Jay Leno's opening *Tonight Show* monologue, and *The Simpsons*.

FOLLOWING A CERTAIN THEME:

Multi-talented Sheb Wooley wrote the *Hee Haw* theme song and appeared as alter-ego Ben Colder in the show's premiere episode. Among Wooley's acting credits are the TV Western *Rawhide* and the film *Hoosiers*.

Taping a scene in the famous cornfield, 1981 — sa-lute!

View from the Pew

It might be the question asked most by fans visiting the Opry: "How did those people sitting on the pews on stage get those great seats?"

The answer is they know someone. Or know someone who knows someone. Every act on each Opry show is afforded a small number of guests to accompany them backstage, and those guests might be business associates, family members, friends, or friends of friends. Guests are invited to relax in the Family Room, stand backstage and watch the show, or enjoy the view from the most coveted seats in the Opry House—the onstage pews from Ryman Auditorium. The pews are available on a first-come, first-served basis, and on most nights they're occupied by a steady stream of people enjoying the show for a segment or two then moving on to a dressing room, the Family Room, the auditorium, or elsewhere on their big night backstage.

⋮ Jana Spicer and Kristin Garrett ⋮

⋮ Steve and Suzanne Cagle ⋮

"My dad plays guitar for Bill Anderson," says Nashville's Jana Spicer, who brought her friend Kristin Garrett, a Carrie Underwood fan, backstage after her father made sure their names were added to the clearance list for the night. Kristin had never been backstage before. However, Jana basically grew up there. "I've been coming backstage since I was three," Spicer says. "Roy Acuff used to hold me up to the water fountain. As for tonight, I just want Kristin to have a good time. I saw on the billboard that Carrie was coming and thought, I better call dad."

—

Steve and Suzanne Cagle from Austin, Texas, visited backstage at the Opry alongside Suzanne's brother Royal Lewis and his wife, Diane, from Madison, Alabama. The Cagles were passing though Nashville on their way to visit their grandchildren in Ashburn, Virginia, and invited the Lewis' to join them in Nashville. The two couples made their way to the coveted pew seating on the Opry stage at the invitation of Jimmy and Michele Capps of the Opry band. During the Opry performance, Steve was recognized for his service to the United States in Vietnam while soldiers from Fort Campbell, Kentucky, were also honored. Fans of Ray Price, Gene Watson, George Jones, Loretta Lynn, and Josh Turner, among others, the couples say the experience is one they'll share with others again and again. "To be able to go backstage with the stars and sit on the stage was just awesome," Suzanne says.

WE'RE AT THE OPRY ~ *Take Note!*

Birthdays and anniversaries . . . honeymoons, reunions, and homecomings . . . or the fulfillment of a lifelong dream of visiting. All are perfect reasons to celebrate at the Grand Ole Opry, and Opry audiences want to tell everyone about it! In a decades-long tradition, audience members jot down notes on anything they can find—napkins, backs of receipts, corners of their programs—and send them via Opry hosts and hostesses up to the announcer's podium in hopes of a shout-out to the whole world that's tuned in to the show on WSM-AM 650 over the airwaves and internet, through WSM and Grand Ole Opry mobile phone apps, or on Sirius XM satellite radio.

CONGRATS TO TYLER BRYAN ON his 2ND HONEYMOON this WEEKEND

Happy 4th of July to George Hauck from Luiseville Kentucky "Where the women are fast + the Horses are beautiful!" ★George served on the U.S.S. Haggard in WWII

Chris Butler & Kayla Cera engaged tonight on the Behind the Curtain tour from midland Texas Congrats!

PASTOR JERRY WILSON 92 YEARS OLD W. W. II VETERIN STILL PREACHING AFTER 60 YEARS

USED TO LISTEN TO THE OPRY EVERY SATURDAY NIGHT AND HAS NEVER BEEN TO THE OPRY.

Visitors: From Italy and California And Chattanooga. We love Country music! Ivan Marchetti Randy Venture Nitca & Alondra Velasc

Kelly Hamlyn is celebrating her bachelorette Party

(We are in the green cowboy hats — bride is in the pink one)

Thank you!
P.S we are visiting from Oregon !!!

GASPER Family
Captain Stephanie Gasper home from Afghanistan midway through her tour with the us army. Still has 6 mos to GO

SECTION-6
✗ ROBERT SMITH
Welcome from Central Pennsylvania!

"The Cousins Club"

Here tonight from Millersburg PA

Alyssa
Mitch
Dawson
Dylan
Benny Bob
Alexis
Scott
Robbie
Olivia

16th
Happy Birthday
To Nicole Cadman from Port Barre, LA
FFA Chapter, Port Barre High
On her way to National FFA Convention in Indianapolis Indiana

---

Emma Mount from Chickamauga Ga is celebrating her 9th Birthday today. She is here to see Lauren Alaina.

Thank You!

To: Opry Announcer

Re: Friday, February 10

Join me in welcoming U.S. Supreme Court Justice and Mrs. Antonin Scalia who are with us this evening.

(Sec 4 Row C Seats 1-8)

All from the same family Brothers, and Sister
3 Couple are here Celebrating 50 yrs. of Marriage
Woody and Joyce Booth from Buckhannon WV.
James and Jeanie Coontz from Belington WV
Harold and Charlotte Booth from Belington, WV
Charlotte Booth Celebrated her 67th Birthday yesterday

Connie + Danny Sexton
1st Anniversary
We Played Martina McBride at our wedding + we are so excited to be here tonight.

Please send a shout out to my husband, Captain Eric Tincher. He is currently serving overseas!

Thanks!
LuAnn Tincher

Guest
Winsome 1st
Vertanner
from ✗ to USA GO OPRY
Rangoon (Yangon)
Burma —
Myanmar

---

❶ 44yr old mother of 5 is a breast cancer survivor.
Mary Browning is here with all 5 of her children, one of whom is also a survivor
KAREN EARICK

127

If These Walls Could Talk:
A BACKSTAGE GALLERY

There are nearly 400 photographs backstage showcasing the countless characters and cherished moments that have made the Grand Ole Opry the American icon it is today. Here's the story behind just a few favorites.

The great Marty Robbins performs at Carnegie Hall during an Opry show benefitting the New York Musicians Aid Society on November 29, 1961. It was the second trip to Carnegie Hall for an Opry troupe. The first, starring Ernest Tubb and Minnie Pearl, was in 1947.

November 14, 2005, saw a return engagement to Carnegie Hall, in conjunction with the CMA Awards held in New York City that year. An Opry cast that included Trisha Yearwood, Charley Pride, Trace Adkins, Bill Anderson, Brad Paisley, and Alison Krauss, along with Vince Gill and Jimmy Dickens (pictured), played to a sold-out house.

President George Bush, here with Roy Acuff, and his wife, Barbara, made no secret about being Opry fans. The couple visited the Opry during Bush's term as vice president. As president and first lady, they took the Opry on the road to Houston as part of the 16th G7 Summit, which included the heads of France, West Germany, Italy, Japan, the United Kingdom, the United States, and Canada, in 1990. The presidential couple celebrated their 50th wedding anniversary at the Grand Ole Opry House on January 8, 1995, in an event hosted by the Oak Ridge Boys. When the group became official Opry members in 2011, President Bush sent video greetings, citing the Oaks as a great choice for Opry membership and recognizing the Opry as "one of my favorite places in America."

Dierks Bentley is joined at his Opry induction by his trusted dog Jake as well as Marty Stuart.

DIERKS BENTLEY: BANNED AND BACK

Dierks Bentley may be the only artist ever banned from the Opry's backstage area before he ever got to sing there. During his early days in Nashville, Bentley had a job as a researcher for The Nashville Network, and he reported for work just steps away from the Opry House. The would-be singer made it a habit to sign up at the office for backstage access to weekend Opry shows so that he could watch performances from backstage and visit with musicians. Such a habit, in fact, that Opry general manager Pete Fisher finally limited his backstage access to less frequent visits.

Not too much later, however, Bentley landed a recording contract and released his first single, "What Was I Thinkin'." The song catapulted the young singer to the top of the charts and was followed by a string of other hits.

By October 1, 2005, Bentley was welcomed as an official Opry member by Fisher, the very man who'd limited his backstage access just a few years earlier. After having been presented his Opry Member Award that night, Bentley held the statuette high, saying to Fisher and everyone in the Opry House, "This here is the ultimate backstage pass. Maybe I could get this on a laminate? I share this honor with these guys behind me who ride the bus. Thanks!"

Bentley says he'll never forget wandering the Opry House halls as a relative newcomer to town, and tries to make himself available to fans and friends when he plays the Opry today. "We leave the door to our dressing room wide open, so people can come in and say 'hi,'" he says. "And if we're not getting ready, then I want to be out on the stage watching the other bands—just remembering what it feels like to be part of the audience. I don't ever want to lose that feeling of being a fan."

Opry member Martina McBride showcased music from her album *Timeless*, a project featuring the music she grew up listening to, during an hour-long portion of the Opry October 22, 2005. Country Music Hall of Famer Ray Price joined McBride on his 1959 hit "Heartaches by the Number."

"Jumpin'" Bill Carlisle was a member of the Opry for over fifty years. Here, he earns his nickname as he puts about three feet of air between himself and the stage of WSM's *Friday Night Frolic* (pre-cursor to the Friday Night Opry) in 1956.

Mel and Pam Tillis duet on the Opry, June 12, 2004. Daughter Pam was privileged to learn her craft at the feet of dad, Mel, one of country's most revered songwriters and dynamic entertainers. Mel counts Grand Ole Opry stars among his most potent influences. "We'd all gather 'round our old Philco battery-powered Majestic Radio in Plant City, Florida, and tune in to the Grand Ole Opry on Saturday nights. Acuff's band were cut-ups. There were funny, and they could flat entertain. I learned a lot from the Smoky Mountain Boys and later on from Porter Wagoner how to act on stage. And I learned from Webb Pierce what not to do. Mercy!"

The Opry's influence reaches far and wide—even over the pond to earn the admiration of British musical innovator Elvis Costello. He made his debut along with Opry star Emmylou Harris on February 17, 2006. The pair covered tunes by classic Opry artists the Everly Brothers ("Love Hurts") and the Louvin Brothers ("Must You Throw Dirt In My Face") as well as the original Elvis ("Mystery Train").

Maybelle Carter, along with her brother-in-law A.P. Carter and his wife, Sara, was one of the most important artists in early country music. Her playing style, known as the "Carter Scratch," influenced many country guitarists who followed. In 1950, Mother Maybelle, as she was known, joined the Opry cast with her three daughters, June, Anita, and Helen, and charmed listeners with beautiful harmonies led by the angelic voice of Anita. Shown here on the Opry in 1956, the gorgeous Carter Sisters put on quite a show – GO!

BACKSTAGE RITUALS

Country Music Hall-of-Famer and Opry prankster George Morgan had a weekly ritual that offered a good-natured ribbing to his fellow members, Opry band, and staff. Each week, he would post his "Ugly List," a much anticipated ranking of the attractiveness (or lack thereof) of the folks backstage (men only, for his own safety!). Everyone would check in to see where they ranked that week, always hoping for the coveted top spot.

Opry members today have their own rituals to calm the nerves and soothe the throat.

• I try to keep my voice in shape, so I make sure I'm hydrated. I drink a lot of water, and before I step onto the stage of the Grand Ole Opry, I take a sip of Robitussin. That's my ritual.
– Ronnie Milsap

• Everyone in my band and my guests touch the brass name plate before entering the Opry House. – Craig Morgan

• The only ritual I have before going on stage is having a couple of Old Milwaukee Ice to settle me down a little. Works every time. – Mel Tillis

• I like to watch the curtain open at the top of the show when I can. Some nights call for a popcorn and GooGoo run. – Elizabeth Cook

One of Morgan's ugly lists from the early 1970s

George Morgan tries his hand at the bass fiddle backstage in 1968.

"Of all the photos hanging backstage in the Opry House, this is one of my very favorites. Pictured here are three absolute masters of their craft. Lester Flatt (43), announcer T. Tommy Cutrer (33), and Earl Scruggs (33), were in the zenith period of their careers when this shot was taken Saturday, July 6, 1957. Lester, Earl, and their Foggy Mountain Boys had endured a 435-mile run on two-lane roads from working a drive-in theater the night before in Spencer, West Virginia, to make the Opry that evening. That month, their band worked 24 dates, did a Columbia recording session, and in two days taped a month's worth of daily 15-minute radio shows to be aired on WSM. For many years, Flatt & Scruggs were the most heavily booked act out of the Grand Ole Opry. — Eddie Stubbs, WSM Grand Ole Opry announcer since 1995

"I love the photo of Randy Travis and me that is hanging up in the hall. That was the night he invited me to become a member of the Grand Ole Opry. A night that cannot be topped!" — Carrie Underwood

"When I see this picture, I can't hardly believe that I got to play with two of the most influential musicians in history. These two men changed American music. They WERE Bluegrass Music." — Ricky Skaggs, pictured here in 1985 with Bill Monroe and Earl Scruggs

Opry members Ricky Skaggs, Vince Gill, Brad Paisley, and Steve Wariner teamed up for an all-star guitar jam to kick off the Opry's 85th Anniversary Celebration May 25, 2010. The performance at the Ryman Auditorium also served to raise funds for those affected by that month's devastating Nashville flood. Wariner says, "I remember being so excited to play that night, I could hardly contain myself. I had, of course, played and recorded with each of my buddies in that photo before, but here we all were together doing it . . . live at the Ryman! The pickin' was fabulous, the audience was superb, and the night was electric. What a memory!"

Senator Lamar Alexander continues a long Tennessee tradition of musical politicians. It seems he takes his political as well as musical inspiration from the Grand Ole Opry, as he recounts: "When I was governor, Roy Acuff would ask me to play the piano on the Opry while he sang 'Blue Eyes Crying in the Rain.' That was a real thrill. Roy would tell the audience about being the Republican nominee for governor in 1948. He ran a strong race. 'I'm glad I didn't win,' he'd say. 'It would have ruined my career.' I grew up in Maryville, Roy in Maynardville, both in the Tennessee mountains. Sometimes when people ask me what kind of Republican I am, I say, 'I'm a Roy Acuff Republican.'"

Opry stage manager Tim Thompson remembers well the October 1982 weekend performance in which the Opry's big red curtain came down at the close of one segment . . . and failed to go up for the start of the next one. After a few awkward moments, Thompson went to the "Plan B" he'd been shown for raising the curtain should the tried and true method prove unsuccessful. While Thompson used a one horse-power drill motor to slowly lift the curtain from the stage, a number of stagehands and Opry members held a portion of the curtain overhead while others kept the music going. Among those on stage were: Opry announcer Chuck Morgan (center, in suit); Opry members L to R: Jean Shepard, Vic Willis, Roy Acuff, Connie Smith, and Skeeter Davis.

In Remembrance

Over the years, when a member of the Opry family has passed away, the Opry House has occasionally been called upon to serve as the site for a funeral or memorial service. While this may seem unusual, the House has proven to provide an excellent location for friends, family, and thousands of fans to gather, remember, and pay tribute to performers who touched their lives with music. Through songs, prayers, and stories, Opry members Grandpa Jones, Hank Snow, Johnny Russell, Porter Wagoner, Mel McDaniel, and George Jones have been honored in the place that served as a home away from home for years. It is perhaps the ultimate honor to be entrusted with the responsibility of hosting as the world pays its respects and an Opry member comes home one last time.

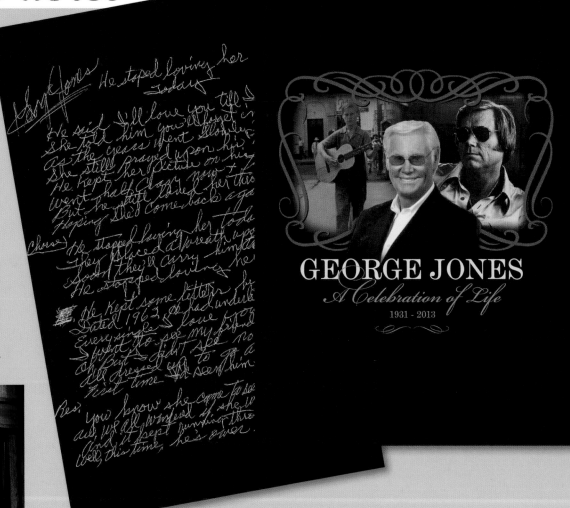

GEORGE JONES
A Celebration of Life
1931 - 2013

A floral arrangement adorns the Opry House during George Jones' service, May 2, 2013.

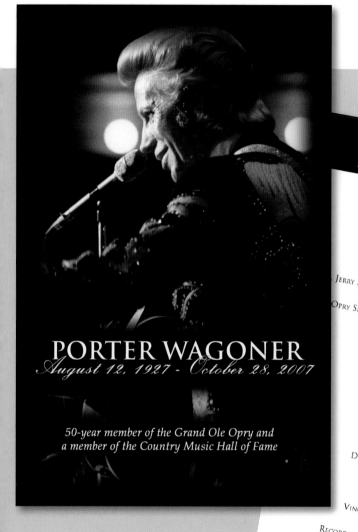

PORTER WAGONER

August 12, 1927 – October 28, 2007

50-year member of the Grand Ole Opry and
a member of the Country Music Hall of Fame

A celebration of the life of
PORTER WAGONER

THURSDAY, NOVEMBER 1, 2007
11:00 A.M.
GRAND OLE OPRY HOUSE
NASHVILLE, TENNESSEE

RECORDING BY DOTTIE RAMBO
"Sheltered In The Arms Of God"

WELCOME
Jerry Sutton - Senior Pastor, Two Rivers Baptist Church, Nashville

VIDEO PRESENTATION
Opry Spotlight celebrating Porter's 50 years as an Opry member

MARTY STUART
"Precious Lord Take My Hand"

DANNY DAVIS, RICK "LD" MONEY, FRED NEWELL
"Rank Stranger"

RECORDING BY ROY ACUFF
"Lord, Build Me A Cabin In Gloryland"

RICKY SKAGGS WITH THE WHITES
"He Took Your Place"

THE CAROL LEE SINGERS
"Precious Memories"

DUANE ALLEN WITH THE CAROL LEE SINGERS
"When I Sing For Him"

MESSAGE
DR. JERRY SUTTON

VINCE GILL, PATTY LOVELESS, RICKY SKAGGS
"Go Rest High On That Mountain"

RECORDING BY PORTER WAGONER AND DOLLY PARTON
"Drifting Too Far From The Shore"

MEMBERS OF THE GRAND OLE OPRY
"I Saw The Light"

CLOSING PRAYER
DR. JERRY SUTTON

Out of respect for the family, please turn off all cell phones and
refrain from photography, videography and recording of any kind.

Everybody's Grandpa

Oct. 20, 1913 – Feb. 19, 1998

WHAT'S THE PASSWORD?

Approaching the door that leads from the auditorium to the backstage area, visitors might be puzzled to see it marked with only the number 51. Famed "Area 51," site of top-secret government operations deep in the Nevada desert, comes to mind.

Now, security at the Opry's Station 51 might not be quite as rigorous as the desert fortress, but the officers do politely, but firmly, make sure nobody gets backstage from the auditorium if they are not on the guest list. With an auditorium full of country's most passionate fans and a city full of aspiring musicians, songwriters, and producers, it is easy to imagine how overrun the backstage area would become if a bit of control was not maintained.

As Johnny Nutt, who has manned the station since 1994, tells it, there have been numerous methods developed over the years to keep the backstage areas secure. "At the Ryman, they used to have code words, like Geronimo,

or song titles—'Wabash Cannonball' and 'Great Speckled Bird,' but people would pass that night's code word around, and pretty soon, everyone knew it."

At one point, colored marbles were distributed to allow backstage access—a different color each weekend—but a trip to the dime store for a bag of marbles was all that was needed to beat that system.

These days, specially printed passes are given to backstage guests who want to go out into the auditorium and back, which works well. However, there are some people who will go to ridiculous lengths to get access. Nutt recalls, "One woman pretended to be having a heart attack and they brought her backstage, but she got better really quickly when she saw Brooks and Dunn back here!"

The Opry Band

THE HARDEST WORKING BAND IN SHOW BUSINESS

Each night before the Opry starts, a group of musicians can be spied in a small room just outside the Opry stage door, running through any number of songs that are just minutes away from being performed on the show. This talented bunch is the Opry band, a stable of some of Nashville's finest musicians whose job it is to accompany performers when they don't bring a backing band, or would like to add a few instruments to augment their sound.

With the ever-changing artist lineup at the Grand Ole Opry, the band is faced with quite a challenge each week. Jimmy Capps, a revered guitarist in the Opry band who first played the show in 1958 with the Louvin Brothers, explains how the process works. "Almost every show, we learn a new song. Today, with computers, management can usually email us an MP3 of the song, and we can listen to it at home, learn the part, then run through it before the show." If it is a song that the band has not performed before, one of the members will transcribe the song into musical charts that each member has onstage with them for reference as they perform the song. The charts then go on file in the musicians' room for future use.

But occasionally, an artist is a last-minute addition to the lineup, or will change a song selection after they arrive at the Opry. In this case, says

Members of the Opry band run through Mandy Barnett's songs with her before a show. L to R: Danny Davis (bass), Eddie Bayers (drums), Jimmy Capps (guitar), Barnett, Tommy White (pedal steel), Michele Voan Capps (music librarian), Tim Atwood (piano).

Capps, the band has to rely on the artists to run through the song with them, and hurriedly write out charts on the spot—"we run it and go directly to the stage."

Obviously, the musicians are extremely talented and very versatile, but they do need a little help in staying organized. This is where Michele Voan Capps, the Opry music librarian (and Jimmy Capps' wife), comes in. Lovingly referred to as the "Opry Chart Chick," Voan Capps is responsible for keeping track of the Opry song charts and making sure all of the musicians have all of the charts they need onstage. Last-minute changes can send her scurrying out to the stage to swap charts before a song is kicked off—just another example of the organized chaos that keeps the show exciting—and occasionally nerve wracking!

Off the Charts
MAKING MUSIC THE NASHVILLE WAY

To the untrained eye, the song charts that the band uses to keep the music flowing look like a cross between hieroglyphics and a Sudoku game, with strings of numbers and a smattering of letters and symbols. But to the Opry band and other musicians who use the Nashville Number System of musical transcription, the charts supply all the information needed for a spot-on rendition of a song.

The system was developed during the late 1950s in some of Nashville's busiest recording studios by vocalist Neal Matthews Jr. of The Jordanaires and instrumentalist Charlie McCoy. The explanation of how the system works can be difficult to understand for non-musicians, but in a nutshell, rather than having to write out a full arrangement with musical notations for each instrument, each

chord in a song is assigned a number. The number stays the same even if the song is played in a different key. This allows for quick written arrangements with plenty of room for improvisation, in a system that can be understood by musicians who don't read music—which many early country musicians did not do. It even allows a band leader to communicate chord changes just by holding up the right number of fingers if needed! The Nashville Number System has become the standard for communicating a musical arrangement in all types of music, in settings from stage to studio, and is perfect for a band that works on the fly—like the Opry band does.

The chart for Vince Gill's "Go Rest High On That Mountain" still shows evidence of having gone through the 2010 flood.

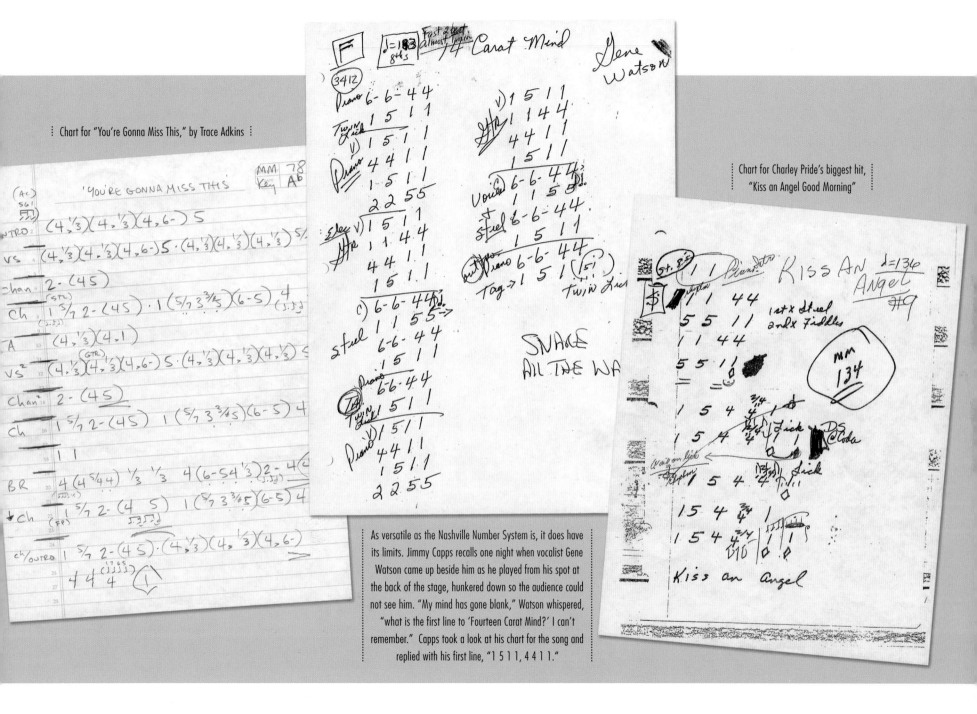

Chart for "You're Gonna Miss This," by Trace Adkins

Chart for Charley Pride's biggest hit,
"Kiss an Angel Good Morning"

As versatile as the Nashville Number System is, it does have its limits. Jimmy Capps recalls one night when vocalist Gene Watson came up beside him as he played from his spot at the back of the stage, hunkered down so the audience could not see him. "My mind has gone blank," Watson whispered, "what is the first line to 'Fourteen Carat Mind?' I can't remember." Capps took a look at his chart for the song and replied with his first line, "1 5 1 1, 4 4 1 1."

DRESSING ROOM PICKIN' PARTY

My favorite thing about being backstage at the Opry is hearing all the bluegrass bands warming up . . . walking down the hall and hearing that music! – Pam Tillis

"It [the Opry] was right up my alley. You go from dressing room to dressing room and you hear all this music coming out. It's like every time you turn a corner it's another music experience." – Lester Holt

As performers cover the gamut of country music styles on the Opry stage, the same thing is actually happening backstage, too. Groups of pickers and singers—some organized and some impromptu—get together in dressing rooms to work up the number they plan to do onstage, or run through a few tunes just for fun. At times, a simple rehearsal evolves into a full-blown jam session with a packed room of pickers and a crowd in the hallway gathered around to listen.

Lester Flatt and the Nashville Grass, 1975

One dressing room jam session became such an eagerly anticipated occurrence that the players started a band so they could do it more often. Between spots on the Opry stage, several of Nashville's most gifted session musicians, who also performed live with Opry members and guests, began gathering regularly in the dressing room at the end of the main backstage hall (then dressing room 6, today it's #11) to play the Western Swing music they loved. Founding member Kenny Sears recalls, "At some point just about every Opry member stopped to sing a song with us. We would have the dressing room full and a traffic jam at the intersection outside." The group decided to make it official and in 1998, formed Nashville's perennial favorite, The Time Jumpers, and took up residency at famed bluegrass club, The Station Inn. After nearly ten years of the Monday night residency, The Time Jumpers found themselves heading back to the Opry, where it all began. But this time, they were onstage. Sears explains, "Everyone had played the Opry as sidemen for years, but to go out there and play as an act—most of us got nervous. It was a very special night."

The Time Jumpers, 2012, L to R: Jeff Taylor, Dawn Sears, "Ranger Doug" Green, Larry Franklin, Billy Thomas, Joe Spivey, Dennis Crouch, Kenny Sears, Vince Gill, Paul Franklin, and Andy Reiss

Wilma Lee and Stoney Cooper rehearse with their band, June 1, 1974.

Senator Robert Byrd of West Virginia saws off a fiddle tune with Opry string band pioneers Herman Crook and Hubert Gregory, March 3, 1979.

Charlie Collins and Earl White get warmed up and ready to accompany the Opry Square Dancers, October 9, 2010.

When Marty Robbins wanted to brush up on his Dobro playing, he went to the master, Smoky Mountain Boy Bashful Brother Oswald. The two would sit in Roy Acuff's dressing room and "Os" would show Robbins a few licks. Robbins' son Ronny recalls, "He spent a lot of time in there. They would be singing, and Daddy would play. One night he [Robbins] did a walk-on and took one of Os's breaks. After daddy hit the same lick for the third time, that's when Roy kind of looked around to see what was going on—but Roy got a big hoot out of it!"

BACKSTAGE SNAPSHOTS

They are friends, just like family, and most definitely, they are each other's fans! This is true of the Opry members and special guests who meet backstage each Opry night. Featured here are just a few fun snapshots captured backstage through the years.

Two of country music's most iconic blondes met for the first time backstage during the Opry's 85th Birthday Bash. Afterward, Taylor Swift positively gushed:

"Dolly is a hero to me because of her songwriting . . . Dolly has just continued to write songs that just blow people's minds! I have mixed feelings about meeting my heroes because I kind of don't ever want to . . . I don't want to meet them and have them be having a bad day or something . . . She was beyond amazing! She was so tuned in to the conversation . . . and really encouraging. It was just a wonderful experience . . . I'm going to write in my journal tonight about that!"

Eddie Montgomery and Troy Gentry catch up with Trace Adkins on the side of the stage, October 11, 2011.

Renowned Pop art icon Andy Warhol paid a visit to the Opry as a guest of Dorothy Ritter, Tex Ritter's widow, and Opry ambassador, in 1977 when he and fellow artist Jamie Wyeth were in town to present portraits of each other to Nashville's Cheekwood art museum. Warhol was enthralled with the backstage scene and commented to a reporter, "I've listened to the Opry on the radio for 20 years. It's a certain kind of poetry they're doing."

When Roy Acuff was asked if he recognized the man garnering so much attention backstage, he replied "No sir, I don't know who that man is. He could be a jailbird or a celebrity or a dee-tective for all I know. Whoever he is, we're mighty happy to have him here."

When writer Wyatt Cooper spoke in Nashville during the book tour for his *Families: A Memoir and a Celebration*, he brought his family with him. He, his wife, designer Gloria Vanderbilt, and their two sons, Carter and Anderson Cooper, took in the Nashville sights, including a visit to the Grand Ole Opry on January 24, 1976. Pictured backstage are L to R: Skeeter Davis, Wyatt Cooper, future CNN anchor Anderson Cooper, Dorothy Ritter, Carter Cooper, Gloria Vanderbilt.

Grandpa Jones, who joined the Opry cast in 1946, chats with Charley Pride on the night he joined the family, May 1, 1993.

Trace Adkins is obviously getting a kick out of his conversation with the Coal Miner's Daughter backstage on a break from taping the *How Great Thou Art* television special on January 20, 2008.

Hampton Otis Turner, age 4 in this picture, and dressed perfectly for the Grand Ole Opry, watches his dad, Opry member Josh Turner, on the big screen as he performs onstage, October 4, 2011.

George Hamilton IV gives the camera wink as he poses backstage with Patsy Cline in the 1950s.

The Grand Ole Opry would like to acknowledge these additional contributing photographers:

Gordon Gillingham	Annamaria DiSanto	Pete Souza
John E. Hood	William Gottlieb	Bill Thorup
Alan Mayor	Russ Harrington	James White

About the Authors:

Dan Rogers has been a member of the Grand Ole Opry staff since 1998, most recently as Director of Marketing and Communication. His other Opry book is *Tune Town Trivia: The Grand Ole Opry's Ultimate Country Music Quiz Book.*

Brenda Colladay has been the Museum and Photograph Curator for the Grand Ole Opry since 1997. She previously served as photo editor for the book, *The Grand Ole Opry: The Making of an American Icon.*

About the Photographer:

Chris Hollo is a professional photographer who has been capturing images as the official photographer for the Grand Ole Opry since 2000. He also works for and travels frequently for a wide variety of corporate clients, magazines and music industry professionals.

About the Designer:

Catherine Hollo has been a professional graphic designer since 1990 and has been designing brochures, posters and other print and web projects for the Grand Ole Opry since 2000. She also designs print collateral for corporate and music industry clients.

To test your Opry knowledge with *Tune Town Trivia: The Grand Ole Opry's Ultimate Quiz Book,* visit the Opry Shop, online at opry.com.